# INTELLIGENT SOFTWARE AGENTS

## Richard Murch
## Tony Johnson

Prentice Hall PTR
Upper Saddle River, New Jersey 07458
http://www.phptr.com

ISBN 0-13-011021-3

9 780130 110213

90000

**Library of Congress Cataloging-in-Publication Data**

Murch, Richard.
    Intelligent software agents / Richard Murch, Tony Johnson.
       p.  cm.
    Includes bibliographical references and index.
    ISBN 0–13–011021–3
    1.  Intelligent agents (Computer software)   I. Johnson, Tony,
1946-  .  II. Title.
QA76.76.I58M87  1998
006.3—dc21                            98-43374
                                           CIP

Acquisitions editor: Jeffrey Pepper
Cover designer: Anthony Gemmellaro
Cover design director: Jerry Votta
Manufacturing manager: Alexis R. Heydt
Marketing manager: Dan Rush
Compositor/Production services: Pine Tree Composition, Inc.

 © 1999 by Prentice Hall PTR
Prentice-Hall, Inc.
A Simon & Schuster Company
Upper Saddle River, New Jersey 07458

Prentice Hall books are widely used by corporations and government
agencies for training, marketing, and resale.

The publisher offers discounts on this book when ordered in bulk quantities. For more information contact:

    Corporate Sales Department
    Phone: 800-382-3419
    Fax: 201-236-7141
    E-mail: corpsales@prenhall.com

    Or write:

    Prentice Hall PTR
    Corp. Sales Dept.
    One Lake Street
    Upper Saddle River, New Jersey 07458

Printed in the United States of America
10  9  8  7  6  5  4  3  2  1

**ISBN: 0-13-011021-3**

Prentice-Hall International (UK) Limited, *London*
Prentice-Hall of Australia Pty. Limited, *Sydney*
Prentice-Hall Canada, Inc., *Toronto*
Prentice-Hall Hispanoamericana, S.A., *Mexico*
Prentice-Hall of India Private Limited, *New Delhi*
Prentice-Hall of Japan, Inc., *Tokyo*
Simon & Schuster Asia Pte. Ltd., *Singapore*
Editora Prentice Hall do Brasil, Ltda., *Rio de Janeiro*

To Annette and Jessica—two very special agents


To Gabrielle for handling the rest of our lives
while her husband worked all day at the office and then came home
and worked nights and weekends on this book

*The overall survival of a species is determined by their ability to adapt to a continually changing environment.*

—Charles Darwin, *On the Origin of Species by Means of Natural Selection,* 1859

# Contents

# Special Introduction

## by Sir Arthur C. Clarke

*Good things of day begin to droop and drowse,*
*Whiles night's black agents to their preys do rouse.*

—William Shakespeare, *Macbeth,* Act 3, Scene 2

Until looking at this book's Contents list, I had no idea what a universe of meanings the word *Agent* embraced. And it reminded me of an incident from the autobiography of my (late) British agent, David Higham.

During the First World War (that dates both of us, doesn't it?!), David's battalion was lined up for inspection by King George V. The King stopped in front of David and asked him what his profession was. He replied: "Literary agent, Sir." His Majesty turned to his aide and said: "He says he's a literary gent, ha, ha." Well, nowadays, as this book shows, most agents are not "gents," or even human. In fact, there are serious concerns that eventually there'll be so many of our "Mind Children," as Hans Moravec calls them, that there won't be room for their creators.

Intelligent machines have existed in literature for a long time: My friend HAL was by no means the first, though he is probably the best-known and most ubiquitous. (Whenever I ask it to do something stupid, my computer says: "I'm sorry Dave, I can't do that.") In 1972, four years after the release of *2001,* I put together my reminiscences of the production, together with thousands of words of deathless prose not used in the final novel, in *The Lost Worlds of 2001.* In Chapter 11, "The Birth of HAL," I reveal that the ship's computer was originally named Socrates (or, alternatively, Athena) and was conceived of as a fully mobile robot. Here's a snatch of dialogue I had completely forgotten but which undoubtedly— though perhaps consciously—presaged things to come.

"Bruno," asked the robot, "What is life?"

Dr. Bruno Foster, director of the Division of Mobile Adaptive Machines, carefully removed his pipe in the interests of better communication. Socrates still misunderstood about 2 percent of spoken words; with that pipe, the figure went up to five.

"Sub-program three three zero," he said carefully. "What is the purpose of the universe? Don't bother your pretty little head with such problems. End three three zero."

Socrates was silent, thinking this over. Sometime later in the day, if he understood his orders, he would repeat the message to whichever of the lab staff had initiated his sequence.

It was a joke, of course. By trying out such tricks, one often discovered unexpected possibilities, and unforeseen limitations, in Autonomous Mobile Explorer 5—usually known as Socrates or, alternatively, "That damn pile of junk." But to Foster, it was also something more than a joke, and his staff knew it.

One day, he was sure, there would be robots that would ask such questions—spontaneously, without prompting. And a little later, there would be robots that could answer them.

According to the analysis presented here by Richard Murch and Tony Johnson, that day may not be far ahead.

Sir Arthur C. Clarke, CBE
Chancellor, International Space University
Chancellor, University of Moratuwa, Sri Lanka
Colombo, Sri Lanka: 18 August 1998

# Introduction

Richard Murch and Tony Johnson have each been working in the computer field for over twenty-five years. About sixteen years ago, they first worked together with James Martin, assisting the author and database guru (seventy-five technology books in print) with research for his book *Application development without programming*. With this book, James Martin defined the new tools known as fourth-generation software. It was the hope of us all that these tools would transform a computer industry fraught with delays and backlogs by unlocking the power of the computer and software so that anyone could program.

It was also our hope that these tools would play a significant part in bringing about an increase in the use of computers. This development would lead to more effective companies and would unlock the wealth of nations so that individuals could, with computer assistance, complete more work in less time and therefore have more leisure.

Fourth-generation languages did play their small part in a number of initiatives spurred by the birth of the personal computer and have helped achieve many of these goals. Unfortunately, what we did not see was that these new tools would help companies increase global business and therefore increase the pace of life. The two insets are personal pictures of our sense of loss in this area.

Have we lost our belief in the ability of computers to help make life easier? No. But we now understand that the equation is not quite so simple. The world is changing rapidly. Despite the problems of poverty, which still plague many in places, the world is getting richer. This has been achieved in large part by the General Agreement on Tariff and Trade (GATT) as well as other open trade initiatives.

This increased wealth has impacted on the aim and reach of companies all over the world. As we read in our *Time* and *Newsweek*, we are now in a global economy. The growth of trade has created a situation in which the ambitions of those who manage companies are constantly growing; and this fact explains the failure of Richard's and Tony's hopes for an easier life for all. In the powerhouse Western nations that are driving the world's economy forward, people are working harder to grow global wealth. This situation is unlikely to change. It will continue.

### The Golden Age of Leisure, by Richard Murch

You might recall that in the early years of the 1980s, there were many technology experts predicting that with automation and the computer age, we were heading towards the golden age of leisure. They forecast that by the end of the century, we would be working less and have more leisure time, all with an increased standard of living.

As we are all painfully aware as we approach the end of the century, this prediction has not come true, and further more, it will not happen in the immediate future, at least in the next thirty years. We have all seen the dramatic increase in the use of computers and have also seen the effect on our jobs, education, and society. But the very dramatic acceptance and widespread use of automation with computers in the factory, office, and home has not lead to any great age of leisure. The technology gurus predicted ten-hour work weeks, education for all, increased security, and the same pay no matter how many hours you worked.

In fact, in the industrialized nations we are:

- Working longer and harder, with more hours worked at home;
- Feeling more insecure about our jobs and the future;
- Seeing less of our families and having less leisure time;
- Taking shorter vacations because we simply "can't be away too long"; and
- Enduring periodic recessions, uncertainty, and fear.

I like to write poetry because I find doing so is expressive. The following poem expresses some of my feelings about this sense of frustration and disppointment.

*The Golden Age of Leisure*

Whatever happened to the promises?
The golden age of leisure is not here.
We were promised more free time,
We were promised less work.
We work harder and longer than ever before,
We are more insecure,
We worry about our jobs,
We have all this technology,
Yet we use it to work longer.
It does not make us stronger.
There is no pleasure
In the Golden Age of Leisure.

---

### The Greatest Nation, by Tony Johnson

In the early 1970s, I visited the United States often. It frightened me. In most offices, staff members "officially" worked 9 to 5, but they actually came in before 8 A.M. and left around 6 P.M.. I came from England where "official" time was also 9 to 5 and where if you stood in the corridor at 4:55 P.M. you would get killed in the rush! I realized that England would never be able to keep up with the USA.

In England today, people go into work at 8 A.M. and leave at 6 P.M.

Recently, I went to Washington, D.C., to visit a friend. He and I rose at 5 A.M. and played hard tennis for 45 minutes. We were in his office by 7 A.M. and left at 8 P.M. (he told me that he was taking an early night because of my visit). By the way, this was Saturday!

The USA is still the greatest nation, but at what cost to family and personal life?

---

Can we make the work more exciting and reduce the dross? Can we get computer agents to take on some of our more burdensome tasks? Yes, so keep reading! We need technologies such as computer agents that can work as our assistants; work on assignments that we give them; accomplish many of those daily repetitive tasks; automate and seek information; make decisions; and do work on our behalf.

Buried in our dream of making programming easy enough for all was the idea of empowerment. What we really wanted was to free the businessperson from the vagaries of an overburdened and often incompetent computer department. A computer department staffed by techies who did not (and in many cases, still do not) understand business. Agents will make this possible, but not by programming. One of the key requirements of these agents is to learn; they learn, in many cases, by example, and all of us can find examples to help an agent understand our needs.

Computer agents will not usher in the golden age of leisure, but they will help us to be more productive, manage our information more effectively, and move towards a higher level of automation with the computers that we use. They will help our companies and the global economy gain wealth by automating many time-based functions and by working for us twenty-four hours a day.

# Agent Basics

*The reasonable man adapts himself to the world; the unreasonable one persists in trying to adapt the world to himself.*

—*George Bernard Shaw*

***Agent*** *A person who acts for or in the place of another by authority from him/her, a representative.*

—Longman Dictionary of the English Language, 1988

Computers have been with us a long time, for almost fifty years. They began in the military, moved to the back offices of large corporations, spread to our desks at work, and now inhabit our homes. There is a great transition occurring in our society, and we are writing this book at its birth. Future historians will look back on the advent of communications and computers, and will point to the intersect of these two huge technologies as the starting point for our new society.

The birth of the Internet is the event plotted at the intersect. There is gathering around this phenomenon a new wave of computer software, the driving force of computers, which is focused on the opportunities presented by this global medium. The open standards utilized by the Internet are slowly penetrating our corporate networks. It is a sad truth that today it is probably easier to gain information access on the Internet than from our own computers. This situation will change as corporate systems and networks align with the Internet.

One of the valuable mainstream tools will be computer agents. These are software programs that are, in many respects, alive; and as part of living in this extraordinary network environment, they have begun to manifest many features and actions that were until recently the domain of human beings.

In case this claim seems doubtful, the reader needs only to look at the stock market, where despite the changes brought about by Black Monday, buy and sell decisions affecting billions of dollars of real money are made every day by the sisters and brothers of these selfsame agents. Such decisions are made by these software agents on the basis of their programmed knowledge. The programming is done by computer specialists working with expert brokers. The software agents that are produced are a synthesis of the speed and accuracy of computers with human decision-making.

In the area of the stock market, despite its complexity, this kind of programming is just possible. As the scope of capability of software agents continues to grow, this kind of programming will not be possible, and a new breed of agents will have to learn from direct experience and develop its own skills. This point is where the "intelligence" becomes part of the picture.

This is already happening. There are already several Internet servers which maintain a profile of your likes and dislikes, and that profile is updated every time you interact with these sites. Gradually the site is building a more and more accurate picture of your needs, which then will be used by computer agents to choose goods that you may be interested in and to display advertisements that offer goods or services which your profile shows you have an interest in.

As we write, the Internet is about to undergo a number of major transformations. New standards and new tools are emerging.

The Internet phone system will gradually erode the traditional phone network. This process will gradually transform the telephone industry as its job becomes simpler; instead of having to provide extraordinarily complex switching to connect two people around the world, which makes up a substantial part of their costs, it will be able to concentrate on providing high-speed pipes. The Internet will manage the switching as part of the next generation of TCP/IP known as Ipv6 6bone, or Internet 2, which is now being tested.

The other huge transition will come in the delivery of video information. Already several companies have huge investments in this new business. Simplytv (at simplytv.net) is planning to provide, in mid-1998, 1,000 channels of TV material twenty-four hours a day, worldwide. By using advanced agent technologies, these companies will be able to insert ads into your personal video stream to match your profiles. For example, if your family has recently had the addition of a baby, then expect to get lots of Pamper ads!

This capability has many advertising agencies in a tizzy. Until now their role has been to develop material and to manage its delivery to maximize the exposure of their clients' products. This new Internet capability, built around intelligent profiling, will ultimately ensure that a company's ads will reach just the people who are likely to buy and use the advertising dollar to maximum efficiency. This process will erode the role of the large agencies to that of graphics design.

*How can your business benefit from this new computer software?*

This book covers the world of these agents from a strategic viewpoint. Section One concerns the key technologies and key opportunities that companies which wish to deploy agents must grasp if they are to succeed. Section Two will provide many details about tools that you can use today. As we have already seen with our "travel agent," this is more than the agent technologies themselves. Companies should be thinking strategically about the way that agents will work with their existing systems and data. If your information is not visible to agents in a uniform environment, then the agents will not come to you, and you will not sell!

Currently companies are channeling enormous energy into making their information available to the Internet via "their" web site. They are locking the information on their products and services to their own front end. But this is not what is required by our future agent technologies. Agent technologies need a way to look at your information as part of a broader evaluation of requirements.

The situation is a bit like that in the old days of paper tenders. In that environment, a company wishing to purchase an item would set out its rules for engagement. We require the following information from you in **our** format. Well, agents will be following this same route, and if they cannot negotiate your information they will move on to your competitor.

Now in theory, agents will gradually get more intelligent and will eventually be able to parse all kinds of complex information, and it is true that your company's information may then be read. But realistically, the entire agent technology at this point will be quite complex itself. It is certain that to produce agents of this nature that can operate globally, tight constraints will have to be applied.

> It is in the interests of all companies that wish to sell over the Internet (which is really all companies which understand the Internet) that their information is formatted and available in such a way that it can be easily accessed by the first generation of these agents.

There are a growing number of books dealing with agents. Many of these books are looking at the coming year, and yet within that year, they will be outdated. Other books look at the technology of agents from a development viewpoint, that is, how to create agents.

This book attempts to give a long-range and clear view of the evolution of agent technology and the opportunities in business that it represents, so that senior directors can factor agent technologies into their business plans and can identify who is doing what, so that computer managers can orient their information content toward agent requirements.

# 1

# What Are Agents?

*Knowledge is of two kinds. We know a subject ourselves or we know where we can find information about it.*

—Samuel Johnson
(in a speech)

## THE BIRTH OF THE AGENT

The first agent is lost in the pages of history. At what point during the evolution of mankind from the roaming hunter-gatherer to the settled farmer, the need for agents developed is unclear. Was there an intermediary between roaming tribes, someone who was persona grata, or perhaps a someone who negotiated inter-tribal marriages? In Sholem Aleichem's short story "Tevye the Milkman," the matchmaker plays a significant role, showing that in this function, "agents" have been in business for a very long time.

Certainly by the time that villages had aggregated into kingdoms, the role of ambassador had come into being. Ambassadors acted as agents for their king and were therefore political and trade agents. In the dark ages in Europe, Jews were not allowed, because of religious prejudice, to carry out many professions and thus were forced to become users. A moneylender would be a financial agent, sometimes representing many money providers and negotiating on their behalf for the best return on capital deployed.

## HUMAN AGENTS TODAY

People have been doing business for a long time. The only intelligent agent whom people had was another human being. A human being is currently the finest agent technology in the world, and as it appears from current research, will continue to be so for quite a while. Unfortunately, human agents have 168 hours available to work in a week. But can only work 84 hours—and at that figure would burn out quickly, that is, less than 50 percent of the global business day.

What are some of the features of a human agent? A human agent

- Is focused on a task.
- Is a specialist with skills that I do not have.
- Has access to information relevant to a task.
- Has the contacts to provide the service.
- Can provide the service at a fraction of the cost of doing it myself.
- Provides a service I cannot get any other way (e.g., being a secret agent).

We use human agents everywhere in our present-day society. We use them to perform services, locate information, and get prices and other information so that we can make some decision or can purchase a product or a service. These agents provide a valuable service that makes life easy for their customers. Many of these services have been developed over the past fifty years.

The following is a partial list of the types of human agents whom we use today:

| | |
|---|---|
| Insurance agent | Sports agent |
| Booking agent | Intelligence agent |
| Travel agent | Publishing agent |
| Talent agent | Financial agent |
| Medical agent | Sales agent |
| Real estate agent | Environmental agent |
| Social agent | Leasing agent |
| Conference agent | Rental agent |
| Advertising agent | Investment agent |
| Media agent | Foreign agent |
| Modeling agent | Home health agent |
| Recruiting agent | Military agent |
| Security agent | Agent provocateur |

This list is long and encompasses many areas. Furthermore, if you substitute the word "assistant" for "agent," then this list would expand even more, for example, medical assistant or legal assistant. The people engaged in these professions make extensive use of computers and have their own systems to manage their individual businesses. Now consider the duties and services that are offered by the agents in that list. These agents:

- Provide information and descriptions of the service or the product.
- Locate the best sources, companies, and locations.
- Find and suggest the best prices or provide a series of options.

- Negotiate agreement between the purchaser and the offered.
- Prepare and distribute documentation, contacts, and agreements.
- Monitor results and resolve problems.
- Provide any additional information and offer clarification.
- Collect revenue, fees, and commissions, or distribute funds.
- Terminate the service or product in the event of nonpayment.
- Send out renewals and reminders to start the process all over again.

What we consider most significant is that the majority of all these duties can be **automated** by using software. Software agents can perform all these tasks and more. Many people will say that this process will not happen, but we have only to look at numerous examples in the past in which similar automation has taken over.

For example, the gasoline retail industry used to have attendants pump gas into a car's gas tank—until an automated pump system was designed and is now used in almost every gas station in the world, thus putting an end to the employment of the friendly, smiling person who filled up your car and cleaned your windshield. At that time, pundits claimed that this concept would never work for these reasons:

People would not be able to work out how to fill up their own car's gas tank.
People would drive away and not pay.
People would always want someone else to do the work for them.

All of these reasons turned out to be wrong.

Looking at the big picture, we know that the Western world economy has made a transition in the last twenty years: a transition from manufacturing to service. It can be viewed that the whole service industry is that of agents. If so, then a longer-term view might be that the Western world is basing its economy on a short-term opportunity that in the next twenty years will rapidly shake out. Those who spurn manufacturing (where goods are actually produced) may live to regret that decision.

In the Internet-supported global economy of the future, a great many service jobs that currently employ thousands of people will disappear in the same way that manufacturing jobs disappeared during the 1970s and 1980s.

In Section Two of this book, we shall describe in more detail the personal and industrial applications of software agents, with specific case studies.

In conclusion, then, a human agent is someone who performs some act on behalf of another that he or she is uniquely qualified to undertake.

## IN THE BEGINNING

In 1964, Arthur C. Clarke started work on his book, and subsequently the film, *2001—A Space Odyssey*. He created what is arguably the best-known computer of all—HAL (Heuristically Algorithmic Computer). HAL, which had to perform a long and difficult space mission, was given intelligence by its creator.

> HAL had been trained for this mission as thoroughly as his human colleagues—and at many times their rate of input, for in addition to his intrinsic speed he never slept. His prime task was to monitor the life-support systems, continually checking oxygen, pressure, temperature, hull leakage, radiation and all the other interlocking factors upon which the lives of the fragile human cargo depended. He could carry out intricate navigational corrections and execute the necessary adjustments to their environments and doling out minute amounts of intravenous fluids that kept them alive.
>
> The time might come where HAL would take control of the ship. In an emergency, if no one answered his signals, he would attempt to wake the sleeping members of the crew by electrical or chemical stimulation. If they did not respond he would radio Earth for further orders. (*Source:* 2001—A Space Odyssey. By permission of Ray Book.)

HAL is the result of the fertile imagination of a brilliant science fiction writer. However, fiction has a habit of often becoming fact. It is the concepts and actions that Arthur C. Clarke devised so long ago that today's software agents are beginning to mimic. If you have read the book, you will know that HAL came to an abrupt and a sticky end when it had to be destroyed because if had gotten out of control and had started to murder the spaceship crew.

Indeed, we have a long way to go before we reach the sophistication of the HAL 9000 series (it was supposedly incapable of making an error)—and the software agents we will design should surely not murder people! The important point is that we have started the journey. As we will see in Section Two, we have started toward the sophisticated use of software agents in space. Arthur C. Clarke has helped shape and direct the future of software, robotics, space flight, and agent technology, and most of all, the communications satellite that he invented and documented in 1948.

**HAL—the all-seeing eye from the film *2001—A Space Odyssey*—is not the kind of software agent you would want in your home or on your PC.**

Another seminal figure in the world of agents is Isaac Asimov, the famous scientist and science fiction writer who created the Three Laws of Robotics. We believe that in time all agents should abide by these laws, which are as follows:

1. A robot may not injure a human being, or, through inaction, allow a human being to come to harm.
2. A robot must obey the orders given it by human beings except where such orders would conflict with the First Law.
3. A robot must protect its own existence as long as such protection does not conflict with the First or Second Law.

We will see whether these famous "laws" play any part in the design of modern agents. Since software agents have already become known as "Bots"—short for "software robots,"—it seems logical that at some point in the future when they become more intelligent, these laws will apply.

## TYPES OF AGENTS

Stan Franklin and Art Graesser at the Institute for Intelligent Systems at the University of Memphis list a number of "approved" definitions of agents, which at times seem to conflict. They attributed this conflict to the mind-set of each player who has her or his own vision of what an agent should be, on the basis of the player's own work in the field. However, the list is instructive and enlightening as it defines in many ways what agents do in the context of the major agent developers and researchers:

**The MuBot Agent** (http://www.crystaliz.com/logicware/mubot.html)      "The term agent is used to represent two orthogonal concepts. The first is the agent's ability for autonomous execution. The second is the agent's ability to perform domain oriented reasoning." This definition comes from an online white paper by Sankar Virdhagriswaran of Crystaliz, Inc., defining mobile agent technology. **Autonomous execution is clearly central to agency.**

**The AIMA Agent** (Russell and Norvig 1995, page 33)      "An agent is anything that can be viewed as perceiving its environment through sensors and acting upon that environment through effectors." AIMA is an acronym for "Artificial Intelligence: a Modern Approach," a remarkably successful new AI text that was used in two hundred colleges and universities in 1995. The authors were interested in software agents embodying AI techniques. Clearly, the AIMA definition depends heavily on what we take as the environment, and on what sensing and acting mean. **If we define the environment as whatever provides input and receives output, and take receiving input to be sensing and producing output to be acting, every program is an agent. Thus, if we want to arrive at a useful con-**

trast between agent and program, we must restrict at least some of the notions of environment, sensing and acting.

**The Maes Agent** (Maes 1995, page 108)    "Autonomous agents are computational systems that inhabit some complex dynamic environment, sense and act autonomously in this environment, and by doing so realize a set of goals or tasks for which they are designed." Pattie Maes, of MIT's Media Lab, is one of the pioneers of agent research. She adds a crucial element to her definition of an agent: **Agents must act autonomously so as to "realize a set of goals."** Also, environments are restricted to being complex and dynamic. It's not clear whether this qualification rules out a payroll program without further restrictions.

**The KidSim Agent** (Smith, Cypher, and Spohrer 1994)    "Let us define an agent as a persistent software entity dedicated to a specific purpose. 'Persistent' distinguishes agents from subroutines; agents have their own ideas about how to accomplish tasks, their own agendas. 'Special purpose' distinguishes them from entire multifunction applications; agents are typically much smaller." The authors are with Apple. **The explicit requirement of persistence is a new and important addition here.** Though many agents are "special purpose," we suspect that this is not an essential feature of agency.

**The Hayes-Roth Agent** (Hayes-Roth 1995)    Intelligent agents continuously perform three functions: perception of dynamic conditions in the environment; action to affect conditions in the environment; and reasoning to interpret perceptions, solve problems, draw inferences, and determine actions. Barbara Hayes-Roth of Stanford's Knowledge Systems Laboratory insists that **agents reason during the process of action selection.** If reasoning is interpreted broadly, her agent architecture does allow for reflex actions as well as planned actions.

**The IBM Agent** (http://activist.gpl.ibm.com:81/WhitePaper/ptc2.htm)    "Intelligent agents are software entities that carry out some set of operations on behalf of a user or another program with some degree of independence or autonomy, and in so doing, employ some knowledge or representation of the user's goals or desires." This definition, from IBM's Intelligent Agent Strategy white paper, views an **intelligent agent as acting for another, with authority granted by the other.** A typical example might be an information-gathering agent, though the white paper talks of eight possible applications. Would you stretch "some degree of independence" to include a payroll program? What if the agent called itself on a certain day of the month?

**The Wooldridge & Jennings Agent** (Wooldridge and Jennings 1995, page 2) ". . . a hardware or (more usually) software-based computer system that enjoys the following properties:

> autonomy: agents operate without the direct intervention of humans or others, and have some kind of control over their actions and internal state;

social ability: **agents interact with other agents (and possibly humans) via some kind of agent-communication language;**

reactivity: agents perceive their environment (which may be the physical world, a user via a graphical user interface, a collection of other agents, the internet, or perhaps all of these combined), and respond in a timely fashion to changes that occur in it;

pro-activeness: agents do not simply act in response to their environment, they are able to exhibit goal-directed behavior by taking the initiative."

The Wooldridge and Jennings definition, in addition to spelling out autonomy, sensing, and acting, allows for a broad but finite range of environments. It further adds a communications requirement: What would be the status of a payroll program with a graphical interface and a decidedly primitive communication language?

**The SodaBot Agent** (Michael Coen http://www.ai.mit.edu/people/sodabot/ slideshow/total/P001.html)    "Software agents are programs that **engage in dialogs [and] negotiate and coordinate transfer of information.**" SodaBot is a development environment for a software agent being constructed at the MIT AI Lab by Michael Coen. Note the apparently almost empty intersection between this definition and the preceding seven. We say "apparently" since negotiating, for example, requires both sensing and acting. And dialoging requires communication. Still, the feeling of this definition is vastly different from that of the first few and would seem to rule out almost all standard programs.

**The Foner Agent** (Lenny Foner—Download from ftp://media.mit.edu/pub/ Foner/Papers/Julia/Agents—Julia.ps or online at http://foner.www.media. mit.edu/people/foner/Julia/ [click on "What's an agent? Crucial notions"]) Foner requires much more of an agent. His agents collaborate with their users to improve the accomplishment of the users' tasks. This process requires, in addition to autonomy, that the agent dialog with the user, be trustworthy, and degrade gracefully in the face of a "communications mismatch." However, this quick paraphrase doesn't do justice to Foner's analysis.

**The Brustoloni Agent** (Brustoloni 1991, Franklin 1995, page 265)    "Autonomous agents are systems **capable of autonomous, purposeful action in the real world.**" The Brustoloni agent, unlike the prior agents, must live and act "in the real world." This definition excludes software agents and programs in general. Brustoloni also insists that his agents be able to respond to external, asynchronous stimuli in a timely fashion.

As these definitions make clear, there's no general agreement as to what constitutes an agent or as to how agents differ from programs.

Stan Franklin and Art Graesser have their own definition:

An autonomous agent is a system situated within and a part of an environment that senses that environment and acts on it, over time, in pursuit of its own agenda and so as to effect what it senses in the future.

Analyzing the key items in this very diverse list shows that

- Autonomous execution is clearly central to agency.
- Agents must act autonomously so as to "realize a set of goals."
- The explicit requirement of persistence is a new and an important addition.
- Agents reason during the process of action selection.
- An intelligent agent is acting for another, with authority granted by the other.
- Agents interact with other agents (and possibly humans when specified to do so) via some kind of agent-communication language.
- Agents engage in dialogs [and] negotiate and coordinate transfer of information.
- Agents are capable of autonomous, purposeful action in the real world.

**We see that agents are, by consensus, autonomous, goal seeking, persistent, reasoning, productive, and communicative.**

Although none of the preceding preclude the three laws of robotics, the lack of ethics as a guiding principle by the main agent developers in the world is, nevertheless, quite frightening. We think that it is important to add to the definition the restriction that agents work on behalf of others, that is, they are NOT self-motivating.

This addition should separate agents from life. This distinction is important, since agent technologies already include artificial intelligence and will inevitably lead to computer life. But as our definition of human agents shows, agents act on behalf of others. If they have their own goals, these goals are not part of their function as agents.

We did consider including the Murch Johnson definition of agents; however, we deferred on the side of caution, preferring not to add any more to the already crowded field.

## ATTRIBUTES OF AGENTS

Agents are fundamentally different from software packages and other commercial programs. They must have special characteristics or attributes. We will delve a little deeper than we did in the preceding list of agent qualities to show that agents must have the following characteristics:

*Adaptability:* An agent must be able to work on multiple platforms, networks, and software operating systems, and at the same time be able to solve technical problems by itself without input from the owner.

*Mobility:* An agent should be able freely to roam networks and the Internet according to decisions made internally by itself about where to find information and data to achieve its goals. It must be able to interact with other agents in multiple networks and environments.

*Transparency and accountability:* An agent must be completely transparent to the owner/user if required but must have features for logging where it has been, what it has done, whom it did contact, and when. Also, it must produce this information on demand.

*Ruggedness:* If an agent is required to traverse networks, both large and small, it must be rugged; able to deal with errors, low resources, underpowered servers, and incomplete data; and interpret different kinds of data, codes, and so on. It should be able to solve as many problems as it can without human intervention.

*Self-starters:* An agent must be able to start and stop on the basis of its own criteria and to decide to gather information using the owner's priorities. The required frequency may be as soon as possible, hourly, daily, weekly, or monthly. The agent needs the ability to decide when to start/stop and when to deliver its results and what interface to deliver.

*User centered:* The agent should act in the best interests of its owner and the preferences that have been set for it—the start of the Laws of Robotics? It must carry out its duties as prescribed and not deviate. But it might have the ability to suggest possible new ways of thinking. Also, it might offer new ways to achieve results or correct ways of thinking.

| Property | Meaning |
|---|---|
| Reactive | Responds in a timely fashion to changes in the environment |
| Is autonomous | Exercises control over its own actions |
| Is proactive, purposeful | Is goal-oriented |
| Is a continuously running process | Is temporally continuous |
| Communicates with other agents, perhaps including people | Is socially able |
| Changes its behavior on the basis of its previous experience | Is adaptive and can learn |
| Is flexible | Is able to transport itself from one machine to another |
| Has believable "personality" and emotional state | Has character |

These attributes are very demanding and require a fundamentally different approach to constructing software than has been attempted before with different languages, protocols, and expectations or results.

## THE IMPACT OF THE INTERNET

Many people consider "agents" and Internet to be connected. The reason for this perception is that agents first came to the attention of the public through Internet agents (such as search agents). An agent can, of course, operate in any environment, even a mainframe with no network. In that environment, it would be limited to operating on the local data but would still be extremely useful. Such an agent might be an alert agent in a banking environment for certain conditions of liquidity or debt. The agent might flash a warning on an officers screen—or perhaps when a stock price reaches a certain level—and then buy or sell.

Of course, as the number of computers in a network grows and therefore becomes accessible, the use of agents to act on the distributed data becomes more valuable. For that reason, the Internet with its millions of hosts is the ideal environment for agents to be useful in and therefore to stimulate the growth of the underlying technologies that make the agents work.

Another factor that the Internet has brought is the ability for agents to act on other people's data. The example that follows of a computer travel agent is possible only because the Internet has given access to third-party networks previously closed or available only to a limited user-group (e.g., SABRE).

In 1997, Andersen Consulting built an experimental agent called "Bargain Finder," which can help you get the best price on the Internet for a CD. In 1997, a new agent, "RoboShopper" from RobboShopper, Inc., could do the same thing for many items, such as cigars, computers, electronics, books, games, magazines, toys, and other items. Current restrictions on these offering are the places where they shop and being limited to internal lists of places to find such items or information. Therefore, RoboShopper will look for books at Amazon, Barnes and Noble, and perhaps another three sites, but will ignore new companies and new opportunities. Another recent example is Jango, which started life as a desktop shopping agent, similar to Roboshopper, but which has been bought by Excite and integrated into their search engine. These agents are not "intelligent" in that they are not capable of defining their universe of search and acquiring new targets. So if a new bookshop arrives on the Internet, you have to tell these agents that it exists, because they cannot find it for themselves.

One area of research in agent theory, as we will see in Chapter Five, is how agents will negotiate with other agents, that is, how they will purchase on your behalf. Doing this will take agents beyond the current horizons of compiling lists to present back to you, into decision making. However, even when all this is in

### Travel and Computer Agents

As the Internet has grown, many of the tasks that people delegated to a traditional human agent are now possible to do by yourself.

An example is travel. Five years ago if I had wanted to fly to Europe, I would have to go to a travel agent. Why? Because travel agents had access to the world's booking computers such as American Airlines' SABRE, and they had exclusive discount deals that enabled them to provide me with "special" prices. They could also ticket me, and then I was ready to fly. In addition, they could find me suitable "recommended" hotels and book me into them, and provide me with a car at my arrival point. With their contacts, they could put together a "package" that, if I had booked things individually, I could not match.

Today I can access SABRE myself through the Internet, choose my flight using a search engine to scan all flights and prices, and pay for it online via a credit card; and when I get to the gate, I can pick up my ticket. The same SABRE system can also book my car and hotel. I can travel via the Internet to Europe and look at hotels, ask questions about rooms and meals, and provide a much more tailored service to my requirements than can the travel agent who has to serve thousands of travelers and therefore has a bland "average" selection of hotels.

But doing that arranging also takes time. If I am planning the family vacation and, like Chevy Chase, *must* go to Wally's World, I might want to take the time as a family exercise to travel via the Internet to Europe, choose my destinations and my hotels, and have my whole family join me in the excitement of learning. But since more than 50 percent of all travel is for business, I might just want it "all handled" for me (incidentally, that is the reason most executives give to explain why they don't use computers).

In that circumstance, I still need an agent. Now I have the option of using a human agent or an electronic equivalent.

The electronic travel agent would ask me a few key questions (questions that if it were a "good" agent, it would store up in an intelligent profile of my likes and dislikes). Also, it would travel the Internet and evaluate on my behalf all the flights and all the options from all the airlines (SABRE estimated that there are sometimes more than 3,000 possible combinations of flights/prices to many popular destinations each day) and would present me with a decision point on the best three options. Or maybe once I trusted the agent's judgment, it would just book the flight on my behalf (after negotiating the best deal) and present me with my itinerary.

How soon will we eliminate human travel agents? Not as fast as some people think. Currently no agent exists that can do any of the preceding tasks.

place, there are still some features that no electronic agent currently has, such as the following:

- Because travel agents deal with many people and are often affiliated with large groups of agents or other corporations, they can negotiate very special prices from airlines, car rental companies, and hotels. They negotiate these prices on the basis of volume. Your personal electronic agent doesn't have this clout—yet.
- Human travel agents (if they are any good) invest time and money in evaluating the quality of packages, hotels, and amusements. Again, they have the advantage that they deal with huge numbers of people and can therefore start to build a knowledge base (which is often not being computerized although doing so is increasing) of the "good, the bad, and the ugly" of options and destinations. Such knowledge enables them to select the best for you. Again, your personal agent does not currently have this broad history of experience to draw on, and since all Internet hotel sites are advertisements, the agent will be taking destinations at face value.

These problems can be overcome. There are excellent guides published by Michelin and Fodor, which will see the opportunity to make their evaluations available online. Your agent will then be able to check these for recommendations.

The "volume" discount is more complex. It implies that your agent has knowledge of, and access to, a pool where all electronic (and human) agents post their forthcoming requirements for travel. A "pool" agent is constantly using the updated information to negotiate with a group of airline agents to get the best price for the pool if all purchasers agree to use their airline. Your agent would negotiate with a group of pool agents who might post potential prices available if your agent were to subscribe to their pool versus another pool.

This is the kind of facility or infrastructure that agents which move into decision making will need, but it is not available yet. It is the lack of this infrastructure that is holding back agent development. If we look at the parallels in the development of communications, we can see that:

- The use of phones didn't take off until there were a sufficient number of users and an effective switching and directory system.
- Corporate networks required intelligence at the node, that is, a PC.
- Corporate WANs required routing, that is, directories.
- The Internet didn't take off until TCP/IP became an accepted standard for packet switching, along with the advent of the hyperlink protocol known as HTTP and the ability to see that linkage simply by using a browser.
- The Internet Web world didn't take off until the advent of Yahoo and the search engines that could find relevant locations, that is, a form of directory.

The requirements for a "directory" in these early communications systems underwent several evolutions. The simple telephone White Pages gives a person's name, telephone number, and address. This simple directory was quickly supplemented by the Yellow Pages, which goes beyond who you are and tries to describe what you do. This is as far as Ma Bell went. Any user of the Yellow Pages knows that they perform only a very basic function. The granularity of the information is poor. Looking up attorneys will give you all attorneys, when you might be looking for a specialized service and so might waste hours calling around the wrong type of attorney. In addition, there is no attempt in the Yellow Pages to add value by providing feedback on quality or information on critical items such as fee structures.

But then, other companies began to fill the gaps in granularity. The Yellow Pages show you all the hotels and restaurants in New York City, but Fodor gives people a way to judge which hotels and restaurants are right for them. Consumer guides help people sort out which companies make the best freezers and cars, and airline guides tell you which airlines fly where and at what cost.

## THE CURRENT STATUS

Software agents today are living in a fairly barren wilderness. They don't have even a true global White Pages, much less a Yellow Pages. The standards that they require to be accepted are still evolving. We might describe them as being the first generation. Until these standards become more widely accepted, they cannot perform effectively. Once these standards are in place, the agents will require tools such as Yellow Pages from which they can gather information and make decisions. These tools must be much more sophisticated than the existing directory structures. The world standard for directories is x.500, an ANSII standard. Like all standards, it was designed nearly twenty years ago when the technicians who designed it thought it would be pretty damned wonderful just to have one computer talk to another. It barely makes the grade today in letting anyone know who you are, that is, a name, and makes no pretense in handling what you are or how well you do your job.

The effective software agent, then, is still a long way away. Can we ignore agents for five years? We do not think so. There are a number of software agent areas where this level of sophistication is not necessary to produce real and valuable results. As we will show, agents are already in use in a number of major corporations and are helping businesses become more productive and more responsive to customers. The astute CEO/CIO or Line of Business manager will realize that unless the company starts to use agents now and starts the organizational learning curve today, many of these benefits will come too late and will require a costly and steep ramp up when they do become necessary.

The final reason for understanding this new technology is that even the primitive agents of today require information from corporate Web pages to be effective.

# 2

# Where Did Software Agents Come From?

*Finally, after spending 40 years using computers as giant calculators, we have begun to understand that their role in our society is to help us communicate in new ways.*

—Tony Johnson, 1996

## CHANGES IN THE USE OF COMPUTERS

### The 1970s

In the 1970s, the computer was being used primarily as an engine to drive large applications that replaced people. This period is characterized as "data processing" or DP. It was not so much a period of support for the back office as the replacement of whole human-based systems. This was the period of maximum visible return on investment as whole departments of staff (invoicing is an example—companies with huge invoice requirements at that time had, say, 100 to 1,000 staff in a room typing, all replaced overnight by a computer printer). At this point in the development of computers, the computer itself was really good at calculation but really bad at communicating. So the hundreds of staff in the back office were replaced by dozens of staff, who would keypunch data into a format by which it could be readily absorbed by the computer.

### The 1980s

In the 1980s, the focus changed, and computers began to reach out, albeit through primitive teletype and what became known as green screens to the front office and the customer. The emphasis was on information capture at source or "information systems" IS. This was another cost saving justification, but now on the huge data entry departments that had grown up serving the computer. By collecting information at source a number of efficiencies were introduced. Accuracy was improved as data was reaching the computer directly not via re-keying. The computer could immediately alert the clerk to any problems with the information by checking it as it was entered. Information became timelier as there was less delay between capture and analysis.

## The 1990s

In the 1990s, this development has continued with the quality of screens—the age of the GUI or Graphic User Interface—has improved significantly, and as the reduction in computer production costs has made it possible to give each staff member a powerful computer on his or her desk. As these individual computers (PCs) became more prevalent, they began to be linked together using primitive networks that initially supported little more than file and print sharing. This period has been characterized as "information technology" or IT.

These powerful computers processing at very high speeds now allowed uses for information that were never thought of before, and the key technology became that of access. Database companies that offered new ways to correlate and access data thrived, starting with simple databases that could store data and form relationships, and moving into advanced technologies such as Data Warehousing and Data Mining, which offer new ways to serendipitously access and correlate information.

In parallel with the increased capabilities of the computer as an individual unit, there has been a change in the perception and the use of the computer. It is now realized that computers have a powerful part to play in improving communications in companies. This process has built on the work of Lotus Corporation with its unique tool Notes. Lotus Notes was the first Intranet (long before the word was coined); and, in fact, in terms of work flow and communications functionality, it is still superior to any other product in its field.

## The New Century

By combining the talents of the computer to calculate with speed, with the talents of a network of computers to communicate, a new key technology is emerging and will continue to be refined throughout the first decade of the new Century; the technology of filtering.

Filtering has emerged as a key issue as the networks have become more open to the application of intelligence; and through the growth of the Internet, businesses can reach out through computers to other business and to the individual. This growth, combined with the standardization of technologies of data storage, has created a situation as we reach the latter part of the twentieth Century in which people are being overloaded with information on the one hand, and yet starved for "relevant" information on the other hand. This decade will become characterized as one of "knowledge management or knowledge technology," KM/KT.

It is this new area, that of filtering, to which intelligent agents will bring value. With the wealth of information available within and without corporations, it is possible finally to do something that computers have historically failed to achieve, an increase in business opportunity and sales. The driver for this, as we have pointed out, is the need to cut margins in order to remain or be competitive. In this environment, only the excellent will survive. This situation means that exactly the right information, no more and no less, must be made available to each staff member of the core business instantly as it is available.

If you have surfed the Web (or your company Intranet) and have tried to find information vital to a business decision, you will know that today this is a slow and laborious task. Even the best search engines deliver to your desk a huge list of irrelevancies that cause delay and suck up time, which is a scarce commodity.

Some companies have approached this problem as an opportunity. Innovations Inc. has a product using Artificial Intelligence (AI) techniques called NewsEdge. This tool searches all the news sources and delivers information to you that fits your profile of needs. Unfortunately, the service is expensive at the present and searches only news sources covered by Innovations, not the whole of human knowledge.

Yahoo, one of the best-known search engines, continues to be top (and therefore to earn valuable advertising dollars) by vetting its search engine results by hand. This extremely expensive operation results in Yahoo's still being the premier site because the results of the search will be richer and more accurate, and thus save time and money.

Make no mistake about it, the Internet content currently far exceeds any library in the world in terms of information, and it will rapidly become over the next ten years the only source of knowledge research used by mankind.

---

Agents will enable companies to automate a whole new set of tasks that currently require human action. By doing so, they will enable companies to limit costs and drive margins down. This result will make companies more efficient and profitable, and those companies that deploy agents rapidly will have the competitive advantage over those that do not.

---

Therefore, agents are squarely in the frame for an explosion of capability to match that of the computer industry. In 2010, conferences will have slides showing the development of agents from simple search tools to human replacements in tasks as wide-ranging as brokerage, management accounting, cash management, customer service, sales, bill collecting, and trading.

# CHAPTER
# 3

---

# Why Do We Need Agents?

*The real problem is not whether machines think, but whether men do.*

—B. F. Skinner

In general, our lives are infinitely more complex and demanding than those of our fathers and mothers. Decisions we are asked to make today at work and at home require greater information content and analysis.

This change has been brought about by global changes in thinking about empowerment, competition, and decision making. Before the Second World War, mighty empires, both political and commercial, were often run by single men or a small clique in London, New York, Paris, Moscow, or Berlin. The war itself and the regeneration of business during the sixties and seventies proved this management style to be faulty. Decisions came too slowly to be effective, and central leaders were often blind to the nuances of local situations and so made crashing blunders. This state of affairs led to a decentralization of decision making.

The new decentralized power, however, created a much higher knowledge requirement in the field. Unfortunately, the kind of knowledge required is not static; rather, it is knowledge of the current, and that is where the problem lies. The "current" has become a big item.

Ten years ago if you wanted to buy a car, you would wander down to your local dealer, kick a few tires, and do a bit of bargaining. Today, through Internet car tendering systems, you can specify the make, model, color, and trim that you require to fit your lifestyle and actually have dealers from all over the country (and soon the world) bid to get your business on price and delivery. Now you have to kick some electronic tires.

It is at this point where computer agents can help, by doing the searching and soon doing even the negotiating. Only when they have completed their task will you be asked to look at the results and make a decision. It is a bit like having a team of highly competent staff members assemble the facts and the options on your behalf—except that these staff members work twenty-four hours a day, you don't have to pay them, and they never go on strike or take vacations.

## PERSONAL REQUIREMENTS

Life is getting too complex and is demanding more time than we have to give. Our personal lives are changing, and our business requirements are encroaching more than ever into our homes. Our circle of friends and the way we interact with them is changing. For many people, the perennial Hollywood joke of "let's do lunch" is becoming "e-mail me."

Computers are now in over 70 percent of U.S. homes. In 1998, the Internet traffic exceeded that of the telephone for the first time. The rest of the world is still playing catch-up, but catch up it will. Surveys show that computers at home are used in a variety of ways from home office, to learning center, to entertainment. They are used increasingly for telecommuting. Even 8 to 6 o'clock is not enough, and more and more people take work home and on trips.

Home access to the Internet is increasing as the accompanying figure shows. IDC (the well-known market survey firm) expects 25 percent of all households in the United States to be on the Internet by the end of 1998. How could computer agents in the home help us become more productive and our lives easier?

James Martin used to tell us back in 1982, "I want a TV which when I walk in the door and ask it, says there's nothing on you would be interested in, but I taped a program for you that matches your interests if you want to watch that." We still don't have that TV, but computer agents plus advances in the Internet will make it possible, although there should be no need to tape anything. Today we are restricted by TV technology that can broadcast only one program at a time on each frequency or channel. That restriction will initially be reflected onto the Internet until server capacity and bandwidth make individual programming possible.

Software packages such as Microsoft Money and Intuit Quicken are beginning to move out of the personal computer into the Internet. As this process happens and as banks develop their ideas of interaction (that is, provide infrastruc-

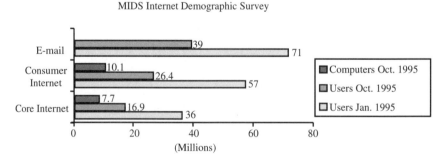

**MIDS Internet Demographic Survey (*Source:* Matrix Information Directory Services.)**

ture for these agents), computer agents will begin to manage personal finances on your behalf, pay bills, transfer surpluses into interest-bearing accounts, buy and sell shares and other instruments, and provide you with regular summaries of your worth. The concept of standing order, for example, is ripe for a major shake-up. The future will see customers' computer agents brokering payments with bank computer agents; there will be no "standing orders" at the bank, and the customers' systems will decide when to pay on the basis of cash flow and demand. There may well be "Standing Agents."

Computer agents in our entertainment world will help us with decisions, provide intelligent quality options and choices, alert supplier agents to our needs, and filter and manage their subsequent offerings. Interaction between our house computer agents and the supermarkets' computer agents could transform shopping. Our normal and serendipitous shopping requirements are easy to understand. Computers at supermarkets are already tracking our profiles and sending "special offers" to our homes on the basis of our likes and dislikes.

Some people are less fortunate in their physical makeup. What role can agents play in making life easier and more fulfilling for them?

## Agents and the Handicapped

*The power of the Web is in its universality. Access by everyone regardless of disability is an essential aspect.*

—Tim Berners-Lee, inventor of the World Wide Web

The one thing that this book illustrates is that computer technology has made great strides in the last forty years. Computer accessibility is something that many of us now take for granted. When we sit down at a PC to e-mail friends across the world, surf the Net, or use an Agent, we assume that we will always complete the task without much difficulty. Although technology has evolved to keep up with user demands for faster and more efficient programming and hardware, an important group of users might be in danger of being left behind: the handicapped. Worldwide, there are more than 750 million people with disabilities and handicaps. This is a significant audience that generally has been ignored and pushed to one side in the rush to make money on the Internet.

Handicapped accessibility to digital media is not an issue that most people think of unless it concerns them in some way. We assume, albeit mistakenly, that all computing needs are easily met. The authors became aware of the needs of the handicapped after writing and publishing a report in Bermuda during the International Year of the Handicapped in 1982. It took many years for architects and other designers to accept the fact that the handicapped need special ramps, doors, elevators, and toilet access. Now we need to concentrate on making ramps on the Information Superhighway.

Computers help give disabled people what they want more than anything else—independence. Computers allow disabled users to "plug in" to a world that might otherwise be inaccessible to them. From the comfort of their own homes, they can do research, conduct business, shop, or converse with others in various parts of the world. The option is also available to enter the mainstream where everyone is just another e-mail address. Names, faces, and wheelchairs are not part of this perspective. In his book *The Disabled, the Media and the Information Age*, Jack Nelson sums up the position: "For the first time in their lives, many disabled people find themselves able to belong somewhere, a virtual community where they can be swept along by daily events, as in any other community."

Besides providing a means for independence, computers also make it possible for even severely disabled people to earn a living. Mark Geisler, a victim of Becker muscular dystrophy, a particularly debilitating disease that makes him quadriplegic, uses his computer to run a small desktop publishing business from his apartment in Brewster, Massachusetts. A specially designed computer and adapted joystick make it possible for him to type with one finger by pointing to letters on his screen.

This example illustrates how profit-driven companies have simply ignored for many years the needs of disabled users. It was not until the passage of federal laws, such as the Telecommunications Act and the Americans with Disabilities Act, that companies were required to make computer technology accessible to disabled people. Although today's technology is beginning to make it possible for disabled people to access the Web, it has been a long time coming.

The passage of these acts has helped disabled users to some degree, but access to some of the newer applications is still a problem because many of the latest programs utilize graphical applications for accessing the web's hypertext interface. Although the access is convenient for the majority of users, it is a nightmare for the 27 million disabled users who are visually impaired. However, things are changing.

Companies are responding to the disabled community's demands for better access to computers. New programs for the visually impaired have been designed to enlarge, magnify, or alter information on the page so that it is easier to read. Another innovation is the talking browser that converts Web pages into speech. The Web-On-Call Voice Browser is advice that allows disabled users to navigate the Web without a computer or modem. The only hardware necessary for the Voice Browser is a phone in which the keypad is used to surf the Net and to request Web site contents in the form of prerecorded audio clips. Users can also request to have text-to-speech synthesis read to them. Speech synthesizers are also used to turn the contents of a Web page into audio form. Users can browse through sites by listening to headlines, paragraphs, or sentences.

### The Web Accessibility Initiative—WAI

The Web Accessibility Initiative (WAI), in coordination with other organizations, is pursuing accessibility of the Web through these five primary areas of work:

1. **Technology improvement.** Improvement that is centered on protocols and data formats, especially HTML, HTTP, and other similar protocols.
2. **Development of tools.** In particular, agent and authoring tools that encourage development of content in a format that supports use by people with disabilities.
3. **Guidelines for use of the technology.** Guidelines targeted at browser vendors, authoring tool vendors, and content creators.
4. **Education of content creators.** Education that is raising the awareness of the content creation community to the needs of people with disabilities as they relate to the Web community and technology.
5. **Research and advanced development.** User interface design, novel devices, certification tools, and labels are all areas where additional work is required before standardization is appropriate.

### Agent Applications and the Handicapped

In addition to all the normal agent applications that we have described in this book so far, such as shopping, searching, entertaining, and filtering, there are specific agent applications that can assist the handicapped. Some of these ideas and suggestions follow.

- People who are deaf cannot hear multimedia or audio events that do not contain captioning or audio descriptions. We need sound applications to read aloud. Inclusion of text synthesizers would solve part of this problem.
- People who are blind struggle with the Web's inherent graphical interface, its graphic-based content, and any Web protocol or application that cannot easily be rendered or accessed by using audio, braille, large text, or synthetic voice.
- People who are physically challenged have difficulty using certain hardware devices, such as the mouse, joystick, or Web controls, including the Web kiosk and WebTV. We need alternate intelligent devices.
- People who are cognitively and visually impaired have difficulty interpreting most Web pages because they have not been designed with this population in mind. We need braille web pages and agents to help seek and find them.

This is only a small sample of how agent technology can be used effectively. The big questions is, who will develop, market, and distribute new handicapped agent technology for a potential market size of 750 million users? One would think that the business case is compelling.

### Concluding Thoughts

Although there is now a place for the handicapped on the information superhighway, it appears that the spaces are limited. The Internet is not as rich or informed as it could be because it is not accessible to everyone. In general, technology is evolving to meet the needs of handicapped users, but there is still a lot of ground to be covered in the struggle for equality in computer accessibility. We need more Web pages that meet the needs of the handicapped. Its all about access, contributing to society, and a good quality of life. Let's get some agents out there.

### Further Resources

Visit these Web sites for further information:

The Web Accessibility Initiative http://w3c.bilkent.edu.tr/WAI/

Solutions@dcomputer agentsbility links to many Technology solutions for dcomputer agentsbled
http://dcomputeragentsbility.com/links/links.html

The Handitel database on dcomputer agentsbility http://www.socialnet.lu/handitel/home.html

## CHANGES IN THE BUSINESS ENVIRONMENT
## THAT ARE DRIVING AGENT DEVELOPMENT

The need for computer systems that has led inexorably to the need for intelligent agents has been driven by cost. If computers had cost more than people, we would not be using computers today. Despite all the complaints about computers, it is this one factor alone, the ability to deliver something that a human previously had to do, at a cheaper and more sustained rate (often but not always faster), which has driven computer growth.

Cost and concomitantly price have driven corporations increasingly to

- be more efficient, and
- survive on lower margins.

If they didn't do this, they fell by the wayside. And let us make no mistake, many have. If corporations didn't do this, they would fail.

The contributing factors to this driver for change have been more open markets and greater competition, which have all flowed from one of the greatest drivers of the human race since its beginning—choice.

It was choice that drove Venetian merchants to provide funds for adventurous ship captains to sail beyond the Mediterranean to find spices in Africa (to save buying them from what they saw as rapacious Arab traders who plied the silk road). It was choice that created that great adventure of mankind, the sailing of Christopher Columbus in 1492. People wanted spices so that they could vary

**Chart of Fortune 500 Top Twenty Companies in 1967 Versus 1997. Fortune 500 Rank Company Revenues 1998 $ in Millions**

| Rank | Company | Rev 1997 millions |
|------|---------|-------------------|
| 1 | General Motors Corporation | 20.20 |
| 2 | Standard Oil (N.J.) | 13.20 |
| 3 | Ford Motor | 10.51 |
| 4 | General Electric | 7.74 |
| 5 | Chrysler | 6.21 |
| 6 | Mobil Oil | 5.77 |
| 7 | IBM | 5.35 |
| 8 | Texaco | 5.12 |
| 9 | Gulf Oil | 4.20 |
| 10 | U.S. Steel | 4.05 |
| 11 | Western Electric | 3.71 |
| 12 | Standard Oil (California) | 3.29 |
| 13 | Du Pont | 3.12 |
| 14 | Shell Oil | 3.03 |
| 15 | Radio Corp Of America | 3.01 |
| 16 | McDonnell Douglas | 2.93 |
| 17 | Standard Oil (Indiana) | 2.91 |
| 18 | Westinghouse Electric | 2.90 |
| 19 | Boeing | 2.89 |
| 20 | Swift | 2.83 |

their diet, in other words, to have choice. It is choice that since the Second World War has driven the General Agreements on Tariff and Trade (The GATT) to open the world markets.

This increase in world trade, which is well documented,[1] has created a situation in which the old-style companies that thrived on large margins are being driven to the wall by companies that can prosper on very tiny margins. The classic example in the computer industry is that of Apple and Dell. Apple's cost of production force it to rely on margins in excess of 20 percent in order to break even. Dell can and does survive and grow on margins of 8 percent.

This factor is important for the growth in computer systems use, because as margins are forced down, companies must do more with fewer staff. The only way that they can do so is by using computer technology more efficiently.

---

[1]Gatt references.

**The accompanying figures show a comparison of Future 500 top 20 companies— many names are similiar.**

| Rank | Company | Rev 1967 millions |
|---|---|---|
| 1 | General Motors Corporation | 168,369 |
| 2 | Ford Motor Company | 146,991 |
| 3 | Exxon Corporation | 119,434 |
| 4 | Wal-Mart Stores, Inc. | 106,147 |
| 5 | General Electric Company | 79,179 |
| 6 | International Business Machines Corporation | 75,947 |
| 7 | AT&T Corporation | 74,525 |
| 8 | Mobil Corporation | 72,267 |
| 9 | Chrysler Corporation | 61,397 |
| 10 | Philip Morris Companies, Inc. | 54,553 |
| 11 | Texaco, Inc. | 44,561 |
| 12 | State Farm Insurance Companies | 42,781 |
| 13 | Prudential Insurance Company of America | 40,175 |
| 14 | E.I. du Pont de Nemours and Company, Inc. | 39,689 |
| 15 | Chevron Corporation | 38,691 |
| 16 | Hewlett-Packard Company | 38,420 |
| 17 | Sears, Roebuck & Company | 38,236 |
| 18 | The Procter & Gamble Company | 35,284 |
| 19 | Amoco Corporation | 32,726 |
| 20 | Citicorp | 32,605 |

## The Impact of the Internet

We can quote Vice President Al Gore, who is one of the earliest and most enthusiastic visible promoters of the information superhighway and is regarded by many to have invented the term. He sums up the feeling and the promise of the Internet in the following statement in a speech in May 1995: "I see American poor children sit in front of televisions screens tapping away and accessing information from the World's best libraries: where physicians examine patients hundreds of miles away: and where everyone calls up a vast array of newspapers, movies and encyclopedias at the flick of a TV controller" (*Source:* White House Archives).

The Internet now seems to have an inexhaustible supply of information on every conceivable subject. To many, this is its major fascination, attraction, and strength. However, the opposite case is also true, in that the quantity of information available is a weakness. The sheer volume of information to search is almost unmanageable. The results returned from searches by conventional search engines often supply information that cannot possibly be analyzed in a reasonable time frame. For example, a search using a conventional search engine such as Infoseek asked this simple, straightforward question: Can you find me a job? The search engine returned 8,604,695 pages. If we allow 30 seconds to review each page, it would take 8 years and 2 months (continuously, with no breaks) to review each page. This review would be a full-time occupation in itself—just *finding* a job!

This example may seem to be an oversimplification, but it does emphasize the magnitude of the problem and illustrates the point and the current technology used. Often we are overwhelmed by these search results and so abandon them. If we look hard and long enough, we *might* find what we want, or at best, we compromise our search or the results we are seeking.

Because this problem is compounded by the dynamics of the Internet itself, it requires further analysis.

### Growth

The Internet is very dynamic and has almost uncontrollable growth. Anyone who has access to a computer, even a small personal computer and a modem telephone line, can add information to the Internet. Therefore, it is very difficult to manage the size, growth, traffic, and many other technical resources required for such a complex network of computers. When the Internet started in 1969, it had just 4 computers. Five years later in 1974, there were 62. Ten years later in 1984, there were 1,024. In 1990, there were 313,000. Today, the figure is estimated to be over 18,000,000 and growing rapidly.

Some estimates claim that a new Web page appears every 4 seconds and that thousands of new users get online every month. The truth is that no one knows for sure and that figures are difficult to verify.

---

It took less than 5 years for the Internet to reach over 50 million users. When we compare that growth to that of other technologies, it startles the imagination:

> Cable television took 10 years to reach 50 million users
> Regular television took 13 years to reach 50 million users
> The telephone took 48 years to reach 50 million users

(*Source:* James Barksdale, CEO Netscape.)

---

## PERSONAL COMPUTER GROWTH AND THE INTERNET

The accompaning table is an analysis of the growth of personal computer use by geographical region over time. What is particularly interesting is the small percentage of personal computers that have access to the Internet—currently only 26 percent of the total number. The questions that now arise are what happens if that percentage increases, and how will the Internet deal with this enormous volume? We will be faced with huge numbers of users in an already crowded and tangled Web.

Again, we clearly see the need for agent technology to automate the many processes and functions that make up our everyday Internet requirements. Sometimes we need see only the result and don't have to be concerned with how we search for it. That's the job of an agent.

## THE INTERNET

Never before has there been so profound a medium that it has had a powerful effect on everyone. Not since the invention of electricity, air flight, and even gunpowder has there been a technology that has been so widely integrated and ac-

**Statistics Showing the Number of Worldwide Personal Computers, 1996–2000 (estimated)**

|                               | 1996        | 1997        | 1998        | 1999        | 2000        |
|-------------------------------|-------------|-------------|-------------|-------------|-------------|
| Europe                        | 9,000,000   | 15,000,000  | 20,000,000  | 26,000,000  | 32,000,000  |
| North America                 | 32,000,000  | 43,500,000  | 50,000,000  | 60,000,000  | 75,000,000  |
| Japan                         | 4,000,000   | 7,000,000   | 11,000,000  | 17,000,000  | 24,000,000  |
| Asia and the Pacific          | 500,000     | 1,000,000   | 2,000,000   | 4,000,000   | 9,000,000   |
| Rest of World                 | 200,000     | 500,000     | 1,000,000   | 2,000,000   | 3,000,000   |
| Total                         | 45,700,000  | 67,000,000  | 84,000,000  | 109,000,000 | 143,000,000 |
| Total Installed PCs Worldwide | 230,000,000 | 277,000,000 | 320,000,000 | 350,000,000 | 370,000,000 |
| % of PCs on Internet          | 20%         | 24%         | 26%         | 31%         | 39%         |
|                               | **1996**    | **1997**    | **1998**    | **1999**    | **2000**    |
| Business at Business          | 30,000,000  | 42,000,000  | 50,000,000  | 64,000,000  | 89,000,000  |
| SOHO[1]                       | 2,200,000   | 3,000,000   | 4,000,000   | 6,000,000   | 7,000,000   |
| Consumer                      | 13,500,000  | 22,000,000  | 30,000,000  | 39,000,000  | 47,000,000  |
| Total                         | 45,700,000  | 67,000,000  | 84,000,000  | 109,000,000 | 143,000,000 |

[1]SOHO: Small Office/Home Office.
*Source:* Gartner Group.

cepted. The Internet has sprung almost from nowhere and burst onto society in a few short years. The factors that have brought about this event require some analysis:

> *The pursuit of the global economy:* Corporations, small businesses, and individuals are now required to seek new markets for goods and services, in areas that they would not have considered perhaps ten years ago. The Internet is a means of allowing anyone in any part of the world who has a computer and telephone to communicate with anyone else and conduct business.
>
> *The powerful personal computer:* The PC has evolved in power, capacity, speed, all while the costs have dropped. The Internet would be available only as a corporate and academic tool if the PC had not been invented, and access and growth would be severely limited.
>
> *Falling communication costs:* The availability of cheap, fast communication is a very important part of the equation. Expect to see costs continue to drop and access speeds continue to rise. The new, faster, and improved Internet or Internet2 that is proposed will be needed, since Internet access speed is the key to future success. We want to access information much faster, by a factor of at least 100.
>
> *User demand:* When users require a service, corporations and entrepreneurs supply it. As these other factors have evolved, people have demanded greater, faster, and cheaper access to information. They wish to see and experience other cultures, to pursue education, and to acquire knowledge.
>
> *Simpler software:* There is a need for increased development and widespread availability of good, high-quality software that almost everyone can use quickly to find information.

The expansion and growth of the Internet will continue to change the face of computer communications as we know it today. This change promises universal access to anyone, anywhere, linking every computer to all other computers. The Internet is not owned by any single entity, government, or commercial body. Therefore, it can evolve in ways that are market driven: what people want, they can now get. Add to this availability the constant media hype about new products, Web pages, software, and new net gadgets that feed the process. The number of people who will access the Internet continues to grow, as the accompanying figure indicates.

### Content

Information is continuously being added at a rapid rate. Information that is not available today is readily available tomorrow, often in many forms. Conversely, information can appear and can change sites, hosts, or servers. Information can also be deleted, changed, or restyled. One estimate puts the actual number of Web pages at over 350 million and growing rapidly.

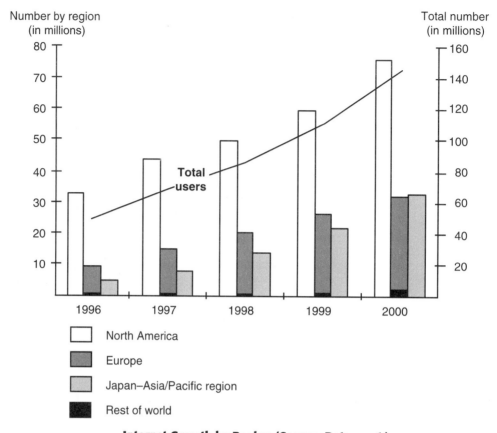

**Internet Growth by Region (*Source:* Dataquest.)**

### Format

The information on the Internet is available in multiple formats. Some information is pure text files, other is in graphics files, and everything else in between. There is no real standard for the Internet (some might argue that the Hypertext Markup language, HTML, is the de facto standard, but this applies only to the World Wide Web). For that reason, it may be difficult for agents to interpret and understand the underlying data.

## The Impact on World Trading

As the information superhighway begins to reach into every home in the world, there will be a tremendous growth in the whole distribution business. UPS, DHL, and FedEx will transform into giants, which through the exploitation of advanced computer systems, will be able to deliver anywhere and anytime at a cost

## Profit Reallocation

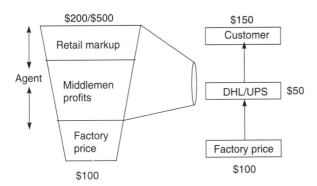

**Profit Reallocation**

that will be less than the sum of the individual profits of the middlemen today, thus delivering goods to the customer at less cost.

This change will increase the pressure on business margins. Currently many business margins are buffered by the gap between their sales price and the retail price. As the middle layers in the accompanying figure begin to shed, the customer will be deciding at the factory gate.

Increasingly, the negotiation will be between the customer's electronic agent and the factory's own agents. Once again, as in the travel business, pools will spring up to maximize the discounting capability. It is more likely that our electronic agent will negotiate with a pool that consolidates purchases than directly. The growth and potential for pool operations of this kind will depend on the flexibility of the factories and their own dependence on "just-in-time" manufacture. There is a huge difference between the capacity of computer systems that factories have today, in which they sell in bulk to a small number of middlemen and their output is predictable, and the future demand created by the direct order potential of the Internet.

It may well be that Michael Dell the president of Dell computers, realizes that his company's expertise in this area of direct sale and support is of ultimately greater value than his direct sales themselves. As we were writing, the computer giant Hewlett Packard publicly challenged Dell to deliver a specially configured computer in one week . . . and lost the bet. Watch this space for more events as they happen. They will.

# 4

# How Do Agents Work?

*When I was a young man I observed that nine out of ten things I did were fail-*
*ures. I did not want to be a failure, so I did ten times more work.*

—George Bernard Shaw

In theory, there are as many ways to develop an agent as there are programming languages. An agent is, after all, a software program. However, for our purposes in this book, we can assume that an agent lives in Internet (or Intranet) space (that is, the agent is negotiating its task on the Internet or in a corporate network) and can negotiate that space to a varied extent.

In the Internet, agents have a more restricted provenance because of the design of the available data, which is almost all HTTP. Agents working in corporate Intranets have access to much more data, but they also face the challenge of having a more heterogeneous set of data to work with.

At first, agents such as web crawlers and searchers were written almost exclusively in C, either straight C or C + + . The situation is rapidly changing, and future agents will be more frequently written and developed within the framework of either Java or Active X. C and C + + will continue to be mainstream, as will Visual Basic, but they will work within a framework defined to allow agents to communicate.

In many ways, the agent landscape resembles that of the computer development landscape some ten years or more ago. There are good, logical reasons for this condition. The environment has changed, and the old development tools vary in their ability to redefine them to the new world. The new world has spawned its own language (Java), which we are led to believe is so in tune with this new world that all other languages are dead. However, other languages have been reawakened from the dead by the Internet, including CGI and Perl.

The authors have, of course, heard all this before. Richard Murch did much of the research for the James Martin book *Application Development without Programming* in 1981, and Tony Johnson assisted by evaluating new languages on the then emerging "personal computers." These brave new world developers were going to "change it all." As our readers will be aware, 4GL languages did improve development, but with nothing like the impact we had all hoped for.

Computer development, as we shall show, has gone through a number of generations. These were defined by James Martin in the books in which he discussed the need for a "fourth" generation of languages. These generations can be roughly identified by their ability to separate themselves from direct involvement with the hardware and software of specific machines and storage devices.

> *First generation:* These languages worked directly on a specific machine and utilized hard coded commands. They made little or no use of external storage, which they had to address directly, and they contained the information to resolve the problems set. Examples are machine code, plug boards.
>
> *Second generation:* These languages could call command functions but had separated themselves sufficiently from the machines to have registers that allowed code to be offset and to access storage devices through separate routines rather than directly. Examples are Basic Assembler—BAL and autocode languages.
>
> *Third generation:* A wide range of more sophisticated languages that could manipulate data and that could themselves call routines iteratively. They usually exhibited considerable control on their environment and storage, and could often run on a wide range of hardware from different manufacturers. The classic example is COBOL, but other examples are Fortran, Lisp, PL-1 (which was hardware specific), C, Basic, and Pascal.
>
> *Fourth generation:* These languages and tools could remove a lot of detail from the coding as powerful constructs within the languages would work out the underlying code to achieve the objectives. They were usually English-language driven and highly productive. Examples are Focus, Ramis, and SQL (which was originally designed by IBM as a high-level language for information access).

In addition to the generations, we should chart the changes that have taken place in the past few years in the whole area of general computer systems development, and then put in perspective the development of agents. These changes have revolved around environments and objects. We expect the development of agents to follow a similar path of generation development; indeed, we propose that we have entered the First Generation of Agents.

## GENERAL COMPUTER SYSTEMS DEVELOPMENT

There have been two significant changes in the world of computer software development that have made an impact on productivity.

### Environments

In the 1980s, if you were developing a product, you did so by typing your program in an editor window using virtually any standard editor, and then you "compiled" your program (that is, subjected it to rigorous analysis and conversion to binary) with a proprietary compiler, for example, Microsoft C or Borland C. You would then test the program's functionality with a series of test environments and attempt to debug any problems. Each of these actions was discrete, and any problems found that required changes forced the programmer to reedit and recompile before testing again.

In the 1990s, this situation changed as the major software houses began to release comprehensive environments for development. So in Microsoft's Visual Basic, the programmer could develop, model, and test all in one package. This ability created several productivity advantages. Since the environment included the editor, the program could be checked (parsed) continuously by the environment as you typed. This process helped in rapid development, as errors were caught and fixed immediately. Also, the testing phase allowed the programmer to modify the program and data values in situ and to continue testing.

Another innovation in this decade has been the growing availability via the package supplier or via the Internet to obtain preprogrammed modules, which can be deployed to develop solutions more rapidly. This capacity combined with the two Microsoft initiatives Object Linking and Embedding (OLE), which allows two programs to communicate via a fairly standard interface, and Open Database Connectivity (ODBC), which standardizes the access of data from all the main database vendors, have massively improved the ability to develop programs.

This has led to an examination of the problems of reprogramming the same solution over and over again. In an attempt to resolve this and other related issues, a new way of thinking about programming and the components that make up a program and a system has evolved in the last ten years, but has only really begun to be seriously used in the last five: This is objects.

## Objects

The most important change that has permeated the whole of the computer development world in the last ten years has been the adoption of the OBJECT model. It is worth examining this model in some detail, as key object capabilities are what are driving the development of agents.

It is object thinking that has led to the whole idea of agent technology. Not that agents are object technology in action: Agents currently are very rarely object based. Lotus renamed a very primitive "macro" function in Notes as an "agent," with no change in functionality at all. It appears that "agents" are better able to sell software than "Macros."

Object technology has been born out of attempts to manage the incredible complexity of real processes. Grady Booch, one of the best known gurus of the object community, argues that it is the very complexity of the task programs we're modeling that created the mess we are now in with systems.

One key to working with such complexity is the idea of abstraction. Booch gives the example of an experienced pilot in a new airplane. He can fly the airplane with relative ease because there are properties common to all airplanes:

rudders, thrust, lift ailerons. Even experienced pilots, however, have virtually to start again when flying helicopters because the abstractions are different.

The underlying concept is one of cooperating objects. It is interesting to note that Marvin Minsky, the "father" of artificial intelligence work, believes that the brain can be viewed as a bunch of cooperating objects.

## WHY THESE DEVELOPMENTS ARE IMPORTANT

These developments are important because the Internet in many areas has led corporations hastening to take advantage of the benefits of the world visibility to recreate problems that had been resolved in the closed world of corporate systems.

The danger is that many corporations are rushing out and starting again without any benefit from corporate experience. This move will be encouraged by the people who benefit the most from disruption of this kind, the software suppliers who see an opportunity to sell new things, and those internally who are impatient with managed development of any kind and just want to buy into the future. Unfortunately, it is quite possible to buy into a lot of expensive future problems at the same time.

We have repeatedly seen the development of a new department, the "Internet" department, which is usually staffed with bright young things whom corporate managers think understand the Internet, and which is usually at war with the internal MIS teams. The justification for this development is that "our computer guys just don't understand" this new technology. It is not our intention to bolster inefficient or unresponsive internal computer departments, but time and again we are seeing corporations moving backwards in terms of hard-won compatibility by creating a divisive approach to Internet business.

Effective exploitation of the Internet opportunity (as opposed to just being there first) will be dependent on seeing the Internet as an integral part of corporate systems and planning integration with the existing processes so that the two are seamless.

## AGENT GENERATIONS

As we said earlier, agents are programs with special characteristics such as mobility and self-determination. But, nonetheless, they are programs. Seeing them as such, we can trace the generations in time using three characteristics; complexity, mobility, and intelligence.

Complexity, by which we might measure programs, is a factor, but is not so significant, since all programs have increased in complexity over time as operating environments have changed and grown more difficult to negotiate. This applies to static and mobile programs. Certainly regarding complexity, current agents are very simple in terms of many traditional static programs. In fact, in some ways, existing agents are very simple compared with static programs. This relationship is logical in that static programs exist in a less hostile environment, and the designers can concentrate on functionality. Mobile agents require considerable programming just to exist and traverse Internet space.

Mobility is a critical factor in the new Internet community. A program may have to run in a variety of environments, some more hostile than others. The Internet hosts run the gamut of operating environments from large mainframes (such as those hosting AOL/Compuserve to Unix and NT servers to Apple Macintosh and Windows 95 PCs. The new highly mobile world of handheld devices increases the operating environments with General Magic and "lite" windows as well as many proprietary systems. An effective agent must be able to negotiate its way through these systems and comprehend their filing systems in order to search out information that it is charged with compiling, or in commerce to complete a financial transaction effectively with security.

Intelligence is not something that programs have had a lot to do with. Traditional static business programs attack a specific set of requirements that are highly defined and produce results that are predictable within that requirement. In the Internet space, this certainty does not exist. Agents are increasingly required to learn and improve. This is intelligence. Thus, the more advanced agents draw on the traditional concepts developed out of knowledge engineering, a sub-branch of AI.

The accompanying table illustrates the changes that have occurred and that we might expect to see in these areas.

Static programs can be defined as programs that were designed to run in heterogeneous environment. These programs, constructed to run in very specific machine environments initially (for example, PL1, an IBM specific language) have gradually evolved a degree of mobility via cross platform development tools.

Mobility in programs that began with Rear Admiral Grace Hopper and the development of COBOL is rising rapidly as new development tools become more and more cross platform. After COBOL, which by its nature was deployed in business application development, C led the way in the operating environment and system programs area by being able to be ported rapidly into new environments. Java is a recent example of a language that can run in virtually any environment.

## Agent Generations in the Future

The issue of mobility and intelligence can characterize agents. The accompanying table gives a picture of agent generations that can be useful in determining the capabilities of agent technologies.

## Agent Generations

| Generation | Description | Year |
|---|---|---|
| 1 | Agents are host based, standalone, and search the Web/Internet using fetch processes. Each iteration of a fetch creates further iterations, e.g., search engines. | 1994–2005 |
| 2 | Agents are host based and combine standalone with negotiation. They spread out into thousands of business and personal functional areas. In the business context, they support work flow and routing, provide alerts, and take actions based on predetermined and calculated events, e.g., order taking and processing that might include alerting other hosts to actions that they must now take. The concept of a virtual company can now spread widely. For example, company A sells products from company B, C, D, and E, and some products made up by A from a combination. When an order arrives, the agent will determine whom to contact and arrange either delivery to the client or shipment to assembly points. Personal agents will filter mail and videophone, obtain bargain prices and alert when thresholds are reached, and carry out research in specific areas. | 1997–2005 |
| 3 | Agents are mobile and highly personalized, but standalone. They search Internet server space and are capable of running on any server. They attach themselves to specific areas and send time-based information back to base, e.g., bargain finders or travel alerts (your plane is on time/delayed by x hours). Cookies are an early and inactive form of these agents. Most viruses fall into this category. Viruses are not much spoken of in the world of agents but are actually the first manifestations of level 3 agents. | 1998–2010 |
| 4 | Agents are mobile and capable of negotiating with computers and other agents. This capacity implies some uniformity of the space traversed and also a negotiating standard. Initially this will be restricted to like systems while world standards settle. | 1999–2010 |
| 5 | Agents employ subagents. Agents are able to traverse any computer connected to the web and utilize resources by negotiation with computers and other agents. They are more sophisticated and focus on solving abstract requests, e.g., what is the likelihood that Senator Grogan is in the pay of the Mafia? | 2005–2020 |
| 6 | Agents can activate and inhabit real world robotics and pursue goals beyond the virtual, e.g., nanotechnology-based mobile entities (miniature planes/submarines, drugs, computers). | 2010–2050 |
| 7 | Agents are self-replicating and can design agents tailored to specific needs. Agents develop agents to carry out their tasks and needs as required. These manager agents are independent, and self-motivating, and in many respects have human capability. | 2005–2050 |

## THE CURRENT AGENT LANDSCAPE

In the context of the Internet space, agents began life as tools to find things. In 1994, Tim Berners Lee and Marc Andreeson revolutionized the staid old lady (ten years) known affectionately by university dons as "the Net" by developing first the World Wide Web (Tim Berners Lee), a hyper-link protocol, and then by creating a graphic interface called Mosaic (Marc Andreesen), which assisted in the navigation of that hyper-link space.

The World Wide Web has become so ubiquitous that it is now abbreviated as "The Web," and Mosaic evolved into the commercial product Netscape, as Marc Andreesen and other staff on the Mosaic project were lured from Carnegie Mellon University to Silicon Valley.

Immediately and with a growth which was so phenomenal that it created front-page news, Web sites began to spring up all over the ever expanding Internet space. In 1994, the Internet Society was predicting that the growth of the Internet would continue until it coincided with the population (see the following).

One of the first problems was to map that space and to discover new Web sites and attempt to categorize them. This step was necessary because if you created a new Web site, unless a researcher knew the name of the site, he or she could not find it. It seems to be the nature of mankind to categorize and label. Most of science has revolved around this need, and the Internet is no different. How, then, to record and track the Web?

## FIRST INTERNET AGENTS (LEVEL 1)

Simultaneously, a number of researchers in various universities began to develop agents that would use the TCP/IP protocols and numbering conventions to "crawl" through every link on every server and to record (by sending back information to home base) the Web servers it found. The agent would then go to all the servers from this list and ask the same question.

The first public manifestation was designed and written by Oliver McBryan and ported to Linux by Stephen Heise. It was called the World Wide Web Worm and was the first HTML search engine on the Internet.

The problem with this idea was that an agent of this kind could gradually suck more and more Internet resources as its growth would be exponential. The first server would give it, say, 100 links; each link would perhaps give it 100 more; and so on. Eventually on its Nth pass, it would be visiting potentially millions of servers and requesting messages back from each, thus clogging the Internet. The agent developers had overcome this problem by using an algorithm to limit the crawler and to force it to "crawl" more slowly and in a directed pattern, thus mapping the Web sites but without putting undue strain on the transport structure.

As the Web has grown from a handful of locations to millions, this general concept has been adapted into a host of very specific agent technologies. Agents began to categorize specific type of sites on the basis of a growing sophistication of techniques, including applying AI language technology to work out what the purpose of the site might be. These agents might search the Web, using well-known compilations of site information such as Yahoo, and then return analysis information for researchers and marketers.

Fundamentally, these agents work alone and therefore can ignore their environment other than to ensure that they themselves can function. Also, at this point most of these agents lived in a host server and used the Internet to get information back to them, which in turn drove their next iteration. Agents do not travel.

## MemoryAgent, an Intelligent Learning Software

MemoryAgent is . . .

IBM claims that MemoryAgent is a true "Smart Assistant". It is agent software that learns about people and then helps them by anticipating their needs and then making suggestions or doing things for them. It also learns about complex processes and can improve them in real time. Plus, it allows knowledge to be shared among groups.

MemoryAgent will:

- Learn a user's preferences, and will predict a user's behavior on the basis of personal history or similar individuals' histories.
- Learn about a sequence of steps and will predict steps to achieve the best result.
- Learn to classify information and will assist in the classification decision.
- Handle new cases and will figure out what to do on the basis of past experience.
- Find the nearest match for a complex set of inputs (for instance, find the closest user like you).
- Give a confidence rating for predictions or conclusions.
- Learn from other agents and will promote knowledge sharing.
- Do all these things even with ambiguous or incomplete or inconsistent input.

Some examples of how MemoryAgent might be used are the following:

Physician's Assistant: The agent learns what drugs doctors prescribe for a given situation (diagnosis, patient attributes, etc.) and recalls a doctor's own practice pattern, giving an intelligent default suggestion. (We predicted this use in Chapter 9.)

Physician's Consultation: The agent allows doctors to consult the practice patterns of other doctors and experts in a shared virtual system. This gives a doctor the ability to find out what a recognized expert has done in a particular situation. (Again, see Chapter 9.)

E-commerce Assistant: Your agent knows you like to order pizza on Friday nights to take home. It knows what toppings you prefer and that you want to pick up the pizza at 6 p.m. It sends an order from your office computer to your favorite pizza shop in time for you to pick up the pizza. It can also remind you that your spouse usually likes a diet drink, and it can suggest an order change, such as substituting pepperoni because it is a featured sale item.

Smart Manufacturing Line: The agent observes what trained engineers do under various circumstances as a manufacturing line produces its product. As the agent spots a recurrence of a problem situation, it knows what to do to fix the problem. This ability minimizes down time and material waste, saving money for the manufacturing firm.

E-mail Assistant: When you want to file mail in a folder, the agent recommends the folder that most closely matches the mail item's subject or contents. It also annotates incoming mail to predict which items will require action or not, on the basis of your previous handling.

MemoryAgent is offered by IBM as part of a custom services solution. It can be applied to many different application scenarios, from individual user profiling to complex work flow or group-based applications. IBM provides it as one technology among many of its others, and it is part of its Intelligent Agent Services offering.

### Technology Behind the Screen

MemoryAgent is a memory-based reasoning system. It provides for both personal and collaborative (social) learning, and is able to share knowledge among individual users and organizations or groups. It classifies cases or profiles on a business task basis as well as on a user level. By profiling business tasks, work-flow processes can be optimized and improved. MemoryAgent provides more accurate prediction than traditional linear statistics learning methods, which are commonly used in case-based indexing and textual analysis. In addition, it has features that make it specially suitable for agent-based learning with little or no administrative overhead.

MemoryAgent does not need a knowledge engineering expert to train or prepare the system for use, or to adjust the "right" learning rate. Only a small number of cases are needed to give useful results. It can also be totally nonintrusive to the user. MemoryAgent is completely Java-based and platform independent. It consists of a core memory-based learning algorithm, a set of APIs, and an architecture for multiagent cooperation.

*Application Design Considerations.*   A MemoryAgent-based application needs to be designed with the business goals of the application in mind, for building the knowledge base and input and output links. There are two main considerations:

1. What decisions will the application be making? For instance, if the agent knows that the usual action resulting from enemy troops' assembling in a foreign country is to fire a warning missile, should you let the agent fire the missile, or check with the General first? Should the agent either delete or put all mail into a junk folder, which it predicts its user will want to trash? Knowing how much confirmation users want or need from the agent is important.
2. What goes into those decisions? Specifically, what actions, behaviors, or consequences will go into defining a case? For instance, in the Physician's Assistant, the case can be a number of patient characteristics, ailment diagnosis, and prescribed drug.

### Memory-Based Reasoning Compared with Other Technologies

*Case-Based Reasoning.*   A case-based system stores all of its data as cases, each case represented by a separate record. This method can lead to large storage requirements and performance degradations in trying to find similar cases when a new case is presented. Memory-based reasoning stores only the relationships between attributes of cases, requiring less storage and case-comparison processing time. Prediction results time in a case-based system depends on the number of cases, whereas memory-based reasoning provides prediction in constant time.

A hybrid of case-based and memory-based technologies can often yield the optimum results for an application. Case-based systems are very good when there is a need to retrieve an explicit record of a case. Memory-based systems are better at measuring similarity and doing recall.

*Open Standards for Collaboration.*   IBM is actively involved in the development of open standards in agent software development and multi-agent communication through its commitment to the FIPA organization, a leading international standards body. More information about FIPA and developing standards is available at http://drogo.cselt.it/fipa.

### Conclusions

MemoryAgent is a new product whose acceptance and success will depend on early visible results. IBM has significant resources and is very serious about the potential of agent technology and about making profits from it.

Our conclusion is that it is too early to predict MemoryAgent's success. We will be monitoring and evaluating this product further as it begins to roll out. It could definitely be an agent that could be successful, if the price is right and it lives up to its marketing hype.

   *More Information.*   More information on this new technology and the way that it might apply to your business needs is available by contacting the following:

   Linda Guyer, 1guyer@us.ibm.com, (607) 752-6024
   Dena Bolcavage, dena@us.ibm.com, (607) 752-1149

## SECOND INTERNET AGENTS (LEVEL 2)

We can find no commercial instance of any Level 2 agents in use today. The adoption of XML (see Chapter 7 on standards) will create an environment in which these agents can operate.

# CHAPTER

## 5

# What Do Agents Do?

*True genius resides in the capacity for evaluation of uncertain, hazardous and conflicting information.*

—Winston L. S. Churchill

Software agents have been around for several years. Only recently have they moved from the hype phase and are showing significant promise in many different domains and industries.

The foundation of that promise is an *agent's versatility*, its ability to make decisions, perform tasks, and roam networks or the Internet to achieve its goals. Depending on the type of application and the tasks they perform, agents' complexity varies greatly. Some are simple software patrolling networks to find an available printer, whereas others are sophisticated programs that navigate across wide-area networks and the Internet, handle many different protocols, and look for relevant data.

Many applications have been engineered using agent technology—in industries such as utilities, banking, health care, and telecommunications—to perform multiple tasks. Key facts are the following:

- Agents will move into the mainstream of personal and corporate computing during the next three years.
- We are in the beginning stages, what we might call the "first generation" of agent products. Future products will include intelligence, personalities, and interactive features.
- The introduction and acceptance of agents will not be easy with issues such as privacy, access to data, and other legal elements that need to be addressed.
- As agents become more accepted, they will begin to communicate with each other in multiagent agencies.

## EARLY EXAMPLES

We thought it pertinent to include some early examples of agents here, although we shall discuss in more detail the features and functionality of these examples later in the book.

> **Jango** is a shopping agent available from Newbot, which allows users to find the best prices for books, CDs, videotapes, and more. It hunts around the net and offers sites that users can purchase from. It was bought by Excite and integrated into their Web site.
>
> **Newbot** is a news and information agent that allows users to enter searches on any subject and then retrieves new pages, newly published content, or information. Its marketing banner boasts "what's new on the net today." More information is at http://www.wirenewbot.com/
>
> **Firefly** is a Web site that uses agent technology to match people's interests in films, music, and eventually other areas of interest. It has now been purchased by Microsoft. More information is at http://www.firefly.com/
>
> **WBI** (Web Browser Intelligence, pronounced "webby") is an agent technology available from IBM. It monitors the use of the Internet, suggesting shortcuts, push content, improved access, and other productivity tips. More information is at http://www.IBM.com/news/
>
> **Roboshopper** is the first "really useful" agent for a home or business user in the area of identifying goods needed at the best price. We will review it in detail in Section Two.
>
> **Bargain Finder** was developed by Andersen Consulting as a prototype on a Web site to find the best price on compact discs (CDs).

And there are many more products and services appearing daily.

### Agents and Bots

As with most new technologies, a whole new vocabulary has evolved around agents. For example, the term *bot* has become common as a substitute or alternative to the term *agent*. The meanings of the terms are the same. Bot is an abbreviation for *robot*, which takes the automation aspect of agents further. Bots have been given specific categories according to their use, as shown in the following list:

> *Chatterbots* are agents that are used for chatting on the Web and are a form of entertainment.
>
> *Searchbots* are agents used for general Web searching.
>
> *Spambots* are agents that are used to collect e-mail addresses from all over the World Wide Web and are used to send junk mail. In Web parlance, it is known as spam.

*Spiderbots* are agents that search the Web for new pages, new Web sites, or new or additional content. They are used by the large search engines such as Webcrawler, Lycos, and Infoseek to locate new content for large databases.

*Jobots* are agents designed to locate employment or jobs.

*Newsbots* look for news.

*Hotbots* are agents used to find the hottest or latest site or information.

*Knowbots*, which is short for knowledgebots, are general agents that seek specific knowledge.

*Mailbots* manage and filter e-mail.

*Shopbots* are agents that shop and locate best prices.

*Combots* are technical agents used for communication monitoring over networks.

*Annoybots* are used to disrupt chat rooms and newsgroups.

*Javabots* specifically look for Java Applets.

*Docbots* are used for locating doctors and physicians.

*Clonebots* will take computer code and change it, making a new clone.

*Modbots* modify or change a program, site, or Web page.

*Musicbots* will seek out a piece of music, a CD, or an audio file that may contain music.

*Sexbots* (of course—it had to be).

No doubt many more categories will be coined as the technology develops, when the creative minds of the developers and marketing departments go to work to sell their products.

## CATEGORIES OF AGENTS

To help in the understanding of the basic terminology of agents and to provide a brief introduction, we can characterize agents by various categories such as these:

- Intelligent agents
- Learning agents
- Mobile agents
- Believable agents

*Intelligent agents:* These are a very broad category of agents and can cross the definitions described before. This is the biggest area of research and has the most commercial interest shown by software developers. We shall examine the definitions and understanding of what we mean by *intelligence* later in this book.

*Learning agents:* These are software agents that basically learn from the user or owner. Learning we define as the modification of behavior through experience or judgment. Once tasks are learned, the agent can then instruct or suggest ways to improve. The learning process is gradual and interactive. Sometimes *adaptive agents* is used as an alternative term.

EXAMPLES:

1. Firefly Inc. is a Web site which provides a service that suggests musical tastes and puts users who have similar tastes in contact with one another. It learns the users' basic musical requirements.
2. The Learning Apprentice is a prototype and experimental software agent for use in pen-based computers or personal digital assistants (PDAs).

*Believable agents:* These are agents that have animation or perhaps personalities that make them believable. This part of agent technology is still in its early infancy and has a long way to go before becoming accepted. In the future, these agents will become more intelligent. The believable agents are now not intelligent; rather, they are versatile and employ friendly front ends to communicate with users. One subcategory of believable agents is the children's toy series of software, or handheld devices known as "virtual pets" (see Chapter Eighteen). Children are required to feed, nourish, and clean up after pets of all kinds in a virtual, believable world.

EXAMPLES:

1. Tamagotchi—"cute little egg"—which is a handheld computer toy from Bandai Corp.

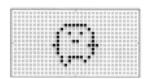

2. Dogz and Catz software that resides in your PC from PF Magic Inc.

*Mobile agents:* As this category suggests, these are agents that are active, mobile, and can travel. They may reside in a host or client computer, and roam other computers, networks, or the Internet to execute their tasks. They are frequently used to collect data, information, or changes.

Transportable agents have several advantages over the traditional client/server model.

1. **Efficiency.** Transportable agents consume fewer network resources, since they move the computation to the data rather than the data to the computation.

2. **Fault tolerance.** Transportable agents do not require a continuous connection between machines.

3. **Convenient paradigm.** Transportable agents hide the communication channels but not the location of the computation.

4. **Customization.** Transportable agents allow clients and servers to extend each other's functionality by programming each other.

## TRANSPORTABLE AGENT SYSTEM

The future of agent technology lies in this area of research. How do agents travel, and what kind of environment will support them and help them function in their task?

Six notable transportable agent systems are the following:

*Active X from Microsoft:* Active X is a development of the successful Microsoft OLE initiative, and developers use Visual Basic or C to develop files with the OCX extension. Although these files can travel, they suffer from serious problems such as a poor security model (Active X controls run on your PC as though they are native programs and can do anything a local program can, such as delete your hard drive) and bloated code, which limits their download in the current 28 K environment.

*Telescript from General Magic:* General Magic has recently delivered a Java-based mobile agent development environment called Odyssey and a service called Portico, which allows access to information gathered by your agent twenty-four hours a day via voice or Internet browser. General Magic has been developing mobile agent technologies for some years but has delivered very little useful code or real products. The General Magic environment is old-fashioned and difficult, and requires the user to work in primary languages such as C. Despite all the hype surrounding GM, there are very few developers of any substance that have "bought in" to them as a future platform. Telescript also requires that all users have a GM server—an unlikely occurrence.

*ARA (Agents for Remote Access) from the University of Kaiserslautern:* This is a university initiative that is not widely accepted.

*TACOMA from the University of Tromsö and Cornell:* This is another experimental university environment.

*HotJava from Sun Microsystems:* Sun is the premier player in the mobile agents league with Java, a development language that supports mobility.

Java is already being used by thousands of developers around the world to develop real agents. Java therefore emerges as the mobile language and environment of choice. It uses Remote Method Invocation (RMI), a key technology for mobility. However, the current definition of RMI does not support key capabilities such as state and data transport, which would be required for real mobile agents.

*Voyager from Objectspace:* This is a Java-based Object Request Broker (ORB) that supports mobile agents. Unfortunately, it also requires all servers to have Voyager.

*Aglets from IBM:* This is a Java-based system that overcomes some of the limitations of RMI and offers mobile agent capabilities. Aglets also does not require other servers to have any special environment other than Java itself, a unique situation that may help IBM gain some ground over Microsoft in the future of the Internet.

*Obliq from Digital:* It is unlikely that a product based on Modula 3 (an object version of Pascal) will provide the mobile technology of the future for the Internet.

*Safe-Tcl:* TCL/TK is a programming system developed by John Ousterhout at the University of California, Berkeley, which is easy to use and which has very useful graphical interface facilities. However, it seems unlikely that this system will form any substantial part of the future of mobile agents.

Safe-Tcl and HotJava are not full transportable agent systems but do allow code migration. Safe-Tcl allows Tcl scripts to be embedded in mail messages and executed at the recipient's site (active mail). HotJava allows Java scripts to be embedded in World Wide Web documents and executed at the viewer's site.

## CONCLUSIONS

HotJava, with the Java language, is clearly the outstanding entrant in the mobile environment arena and will continue to dominate this area. RMI will mature and will challenge CORBA and the Open Systems group for dominance in the future mobile world.

### Key to Success

The key to success for business is clearly the second generation environment and the development of the tools inhouse to create the negotiating agents that allow the external world to access your corporation's information.

# 6

# Who Are the Players?

*Unless commitment is made, there are only promises and hopes; but no plans.*

—Peter F. Drucker

## INTRODUCTION

Before we examine the main players in the agent software market, it is pertinent to review some basic facts about the software industry. The world software market is one of the most dynamic and innovative sectors of the global economy. It is difficult to compare the growth of such an industry with that of others.

In the United States, which is considered to be the center of the global software industry, the growth between 1990 and 1996 grew at the extraordinary rate of 12.5 percent annually. This is two-and-a-half times the growth rate of the U.S. economy as a whole. It is an industry that employs over 2 million people, with compensation of above-average salaries in more than 44,000 companies generating revenues of over $100 billion. This kind of growth is expected to continue and to accelerate even further as we enter the new millenium. Technologies that contribute to the explosive growth of the Internet have contributed to and will sustain that growth, together with the need to conduct business on a global scale. It is a glamorous industry that attracts entrepreneurs who have ideas, enthusiasm, energy . . . and a garage in which to start.

This phenomenal growth has not gone unnoticed. Alan Greenspan, the powerful chairman of the Federal Reserve, had this to say:

> The dramatic improvements in computing power and communication and information technology appear to have been a major force behind increasing productivity. Those innovations, together with fierce competitive pressures in our high-tech industries, to make them available to as many homes, offices, stores and shop floors as possible, have produced double-digit annual reductions in prices of capital goods embodying new technologies.
>
> Indeed, many products considered to be at the cutting edge of technology as recently as two to three years ago have become so standardized and in-

expensive that they have achieved near-commodity status, a development that has allowed businesses to accelerate their accumulation of more and better capital. *(Testimony of Alan Greenspan before the Subcommittee on Domestic and International Monetary Policy of the House Banking and Financial Services Committee in Washington, D.C., February 24, 1998.)*

Emerging countries such as India, China, and Singapore have developed thriving software industries providing significant economic growth, and these countries contribute fully to the global software market.

## The Types of Software

In this section we will discuss the two main questions about the development of agent software, which are:

- What types of software are available?
- Who are the players, and what are some examples?

Basically, there are *six types of on environments for developing agents.*

1. **Languages.** This is the most basic approach as with any other type of software. Early developers have been using a variety of languages such as C and C++. Basic Assembler Language, BAL, has been used for prototypes and experimental products but is being phased out as better tools emerge. Java is the latest entrant and shows much promise because of its portability. Other leading languages are Telescript and TCL. Microsoft's Active X will become popular. Languages have the benefit of much greater flexibility and are at the high end of the agent food chain.

   VENDOR EXAMPLES:

   Microsoft, Inc.
   General Magic, Inc.
   Sun, Inc.
   Vertel, Inc.
   Agentsoft, Inc.
   First Virtual Holdings, Inc.

2. **Development environments.** Vendors are beginning to provide complete environments to generate complex agents. Such software includes a full set of tools such as editors, debugging aids, graphical interface generators, and code validation tools. This type is still in its infancy and requires substantial resources from the vendor to generate the complete line of software required. IBM is an example with its Agent Building Environment, ABE.

VENDOR EXAMPLES:

> Gensym, Inc.
> IBM, Inc.
> Blackboard Technology
> TMN Agent Development Environment
> Lotus Development Corp.
> Neuron Data, Inc.

3. **Class libraries.** These are additional facilities used by languages. The simple definition is that class libraries can be considered as agent building blocks and have a wide variety of functionality. Reuse is the name of the game.

VENDOR EXAMPLES:

> AgentSoft, Inc.
> IBM, Inc.
> General Magic, Inc.
> Objectspace, Inc.
> FTP Software, Inc.
> Crystaliz, Inc.

4. **Personalization.** Software tools are now provided that give agents the capability of personalization, such as filtering news, and linking e-mail and links to calendar suites as examples. This software is spun off as a separate category altogether as vendors see a new market for targeting personalization engines for Internet Web development.

VENDOR EXAMPLES:

> Broadvision, Inc.
> Guideware, Inc.
> Agnetsoft, Inc.
> Wisewire, Inc.
> Aptex, Inc.
> Vignette, Inc.
> Firefly, Inc.

5. **Research & development.** Many companies have confined their interest to watching the market and developments. Others with large amounts of resources are conducting very large development programs to compete in the global agent market.

VENDOR EXAMPLES:

> Oracle, Inc.
> Digital Equipment Corp.
> AT&T

> Apple Computer, Inc.
> Logica, Ltd.
> Siemens

6. **All the rest.** This is a catchall category that contains very specific tools for agent management, knowledge management, and network and interface communication.

   VENDOR EXAMPLES:

> Edify, Inc.
> Verity, Inc.
> Microsoft, Inc.
> BMC, Inc.
> Systemsoft, Inc.
> Sun Soft, Inc.
> Charles River Analytics
> Comshare, Inc.
> MicroStrategy, Inc.
> Quasar, Inc.
> Bellcore, Inc.

## Conclusion

The key question is how much of the agent software will industry contribute to the huge revenues we discussed at the beginning of this Chapter? The answer is unknown: The jury is out. It will be dependent on how users everywhere accept agent technology and the marketplace itself. "If you build it, they will come." Other questions are, who will survive, and when will be the agent shakeout as there has been with other technologies, for example CASE? Again, too early to tell.

## LEADING ACADEMIC INSTITUTIONS

The following list is an attempt to include some of the leading academic institutions that are conducting and developing agent technology today.

- University of California at Berkeley has many agent programs, research, and a particular interest in mobile agent development. Anderson College at U.C., which was very involved in predictive software in the 1980s, has applied this knowledge to agents. Professor Arthur Geoffrion is leading a team in this area.
- Carnegie Mellon, Pittsburgh, Pennsylvania, provides agent technology in many of its seven colleges and more than sixty research centers.

- Dartmouth College, New Hampshire, has several research programs including AgentTcl, a scripting language.
- Massachusetts Institute of Technology Artificial Intelligence Laboratory, Cambridge, Massachusetts, is the home of Pattie Maes, a pioneer in agents who has been active with numerous programs. It also has strategic alliances with IBM.
- MIT Media Laboratory has been a cornerstone for emerging technologies and integrates agent technology with TV, Internet, and other media.
- University of North Carolina at Chapel Hill does research on intelligent multimedia technologies, including 3D animation and knowledge-based learning environments, populated by intelligent animated agents.
- The Distributed AI Unit at Queen Mary & Westfield College, University of London, United Kingdom.
- Stanford University, California, provides basic agent functionality packaged as a Java application or applet. It also allows agent interaction via exchange of KQML messages.
- University of Maryland, College Park, UMASS Distributed Artificial Intelligence produces a monthly newsletter, mailing list, and lots of information by Professor Tim Finnin.
- University of Washington, Seattle, has a variety of research products (Softbots) and services through their programs.
- Worcester Polytechnic Institute Artificial Intelligence Research Group (AIRG) is based in the United Kingdom. AIRG members share interests in the theory and applications of knowledge-based systems. Current and recent research interests include knowledge-based design, multiagent systems, machine learning, and intelligent interfaces.
- Cambridge University, United Kingdom, has a comprehensive repository for information about research into fields of AI concerning computer agents.

### Other Academic Web Pages, Conferences, and Places of Agent Interest

#### ACADEMIC WEB PAGES
Computer agents (Cambridge, U.K.)
http://www.cl.cam.ac.uk/users/rwab1/agents.html

UMBC Computer agents (Finin)
http://www.cs.umbc.edu/agents/

Collected Agent Information (Birmingham, U.K.)
http://www.cs.bham.ac.uk/~amw/agents/index.html

The@gency (Normandy, France)
http://www.info.unicaen.fr/~serge/sma.html

Aberdeen Agents Page (U.K.) (Software Agents)
http://www.csd.abdn.ac.uk/~pedwards/agents.html

Intelligent Agents (collected information)
http://elf.kaist.ac.kr/~bhkim/agents/index.html

The Software Agents Mailing List
http://www.smli.com/research/tcl/lists/agents-list.html

Learning in Multi-Agent Systems Webliography
http://dis.cs.umass.edu/research/agents-learn.html

NetWatch Top Ten—Intelligent Agents / Information Agents
http://www.pulver.com/netwatch/topten/tt9.htm

Intelligent Agents
http://www.primenet.com/~terry/New_Home_Page/ai_info/intelligent_agents.html

The Agent Society
http://www.agent.org/

Autonomous Agents'97: Related Sites—a conference on agents
http://www.isi.edu/isd/AA97/related-sites.html

The Mining Company Software Agents Guide—an excellent site with a multitude of
   information
http://softwareagents.miningco.com/

UMass Distributed Artificial Intelligence Laboratory
http://dis.cs.umass.edu/

DAI Research Unit (Queen Mary & Westfield College, London, U.K.)
http://www.elec.qmw.ac.uk/dai/

Software Agents Group, MIT Media Lab
http://agents.www.media.mit.edu/groups/agents/

UNH Cooperative Distributed Problem-Solving Research Group
http://cdps.cs.unh.edu/

WPI Single Function Agent Research
http://www.cs.wpi.edu/Research/aidg/SiFA/sifa.html

Stanford Next-Link Project
http://cdr.stanford.edu/html/NextLink/NextLink.html

Mutli-agent systems (Brandeis University, Waltham, Massachusetts)
http://www.cs.brandeis.edu/dept/faculty/mataric/

Multi-Agent Systems in Geneva, Switzerland
http://expasy.hcuge.ch/sgaico/html/olb/baujard.html

MIT Media Lab Autonomous Agents Group
http://agents.www.media.mit.edu/groups/agents/

Collaborative Interface Agents
http://agents.www.media.mit.edu/groups/agents/papers/aaai-ymp/aaai.html

Architectures for Intelligent Agents (Birmingham, U.K.)
http://www.cs.bham.ac.uk/~axs/cogaff.html

MAGMA: Modelling Autonomous aGents in a Multi-Agent world (IMAG, Grenoble, France)
http://cosmos.imag.fr/MAGMA/home-fr.html

DAI-hards at University of Tulsa, Oklahoma
http://euler.mcs.utulsa.edu/~sandip/sandip.html

DAI at Hebrew University, Jerusalem, Israel
http://www.cs.huji.ac.il/labs/dai/

Index of MAAMAW
http://www.cs.umbc.edu/agents/maamaw/

The Internet Softbot at Washington State University
http://www.cs.washington.edu/research/projects/softbots/www/

AgentX project (Cornell DRI)
http://www.tc.cornell.edu/er/sci93/dis14agent/dis14agent.html

FIPA: The Foundation for Intelligent Physical Agents
http://drogo.cselt.stet.it/ufv/leonardo/fipa.htm

CSCW Directory (extensive)
http://www.demon.co.uk/jrac/cscwdir.html

The BotSpot
http://www.botspot.com/newbots/

Knowledge Sharing Technology: A Quick Summary from Stanford
http://www-ksl.stanford.edu/kst/kst-overview.html

Knowledge Sharing Effort (Logic Group)
http://logic.stanford.edu/knowledge.html

ARPA Knowledge Sharing Effort public library
http://www-ksl.stanford.edu/knowledge-sharing/README.html

KQML—Knowledge Query and Manipulation Language
http://retriever.cs.umbc.edu/kqml/

Knowledge Interchange Format
http:www.cs.umbc.edu/kse/kif.html

Ontology: A Resource Page from the University of Ottawa
http://www.csi.uottawa.ca:80/dept/Ontology/

Ontology resources & conferences
http://mnemosyne.itc.it:1024/ontology.html

About the KACTUS toolkit
http://www.swi.psy.uva.nl/projects/Kactus/toolkit/about.html

Negotiation Bibliography
http://www.business.carleton.ca/interneg/reference/bibliography.html

## Places of Agent Interest

### CONFERENCES

WWW Virtual Library: Conferences—Agents (a huge resource)
http://www.iao.fhg.de/Library/conferences/index/Agents.html

Agents/KQML Calendar of Events, conferences
http://www.cs.umbc.edu:80/kqml/events/

Agent's World (incl. ICMAS'98)
http://goma.univ-paris13.fr/AgentsWorld/

Agents '98—a conference and its proceedings
http://www.cis.udel.edu/~agents98/

PAAM'97 (Practical Applications of Intelligent Agents and Multi-Agents)
http://www.demon.co.uk/ar/PAAM97/index.html

First Australian Workshop of DAI
http://walrus.adfa.oz.au/ai95/w03.html

International Conference on Multiagent Systems (ICMAS)
http://icmas.cs.umass.edu/ICMAS/ (1995)
http://www.keihanna-plaza.co.jp/ICMAS96/index.html (1996)

Workshop on Decentralized Intelligent and Multi-Agent Systems (DIMAS'95)
http://www.agh.edu.pl/~dimas95k/

CIKM-94 Intelligent Information Agents Workshop
http://www.cs.umbc.edu/~cikm/1994/iia/

IJCAI95 Agent Theories, Architectures & Languages Workshop
http://www.doc.mmu.ac.uk/STAFF/mike/atal95.html

IJCIA95 Workshop on Adaptation & Learning in Multiagent Systems
http://euler.mcs.utulsa.edu/~sandip/wshop/schedule.html

AAAI-97 Workshop on Multiagent Learning (July 1997)
http://euler.mcs.utulsa.edu/~sandip/wshop/97/

Adaptation, Co-evolution and Learning in Multiagent Systems (AAAI-96 Spring
   Symp.)
http://euler.mcs.utulsa.edu/~sandip/ss.html

Second International Conference on the Design of Cooperative Systems (COOP'96)
http://www.cs.wpi.edu/Research/aidg/CFPapers/COOP96.html

Call for papers: Complete Agent Learning In Complex Environments
http://www.cs.brandeis.edu/~maja/abj-special-issue/

Cooperative Information Agents CIA-96 Workshop
http://www.informatki.uni-kiel.de/~mkl/cia97.html

MAAMAW '96: 7th European Wkshp on Modelling Autonomous Agents in a Multi-
   Agent World
http://arti.vub.ac.be/www/maamaw/welcome.html

2nd Knowledge Engineering Forum: DISTRIBUTED EXPERTISE
http://wwwagr.informatik.uni-kl.de/~keforum/

AAAI-96 International Workshop on Intelligent Adaptive Agents (IAA-96)
http://www.aaai.org/conferences/
Call for Papers and Call for Participants
Discussion topics and Final Program

ECAI-96 Workshops
http://www.dfki.uni-sb.de/ecai96/accepted-workshops.html
   Learning in Distributed Artificial Intelligence Systems
   Modelling Conflicts in AI
   Agent Theories, Architectures and Languages
   Argumentation in Agent Communication
   Intelligent Agents for Telcoms Applications

AAAI-97 Workshop on Multiagent Learning
http://www.aaai.org/Workshops/

Adaption and Learning in Multi-Agent Systems (1996)
http://wwwbrauer.informatik.tu-muenchen.de/~weissg/LNAI-1042/

Distributed artificial intelligence meets machine learning (1997)
http://www7.informatik.tu-muenchen.de/~weissg/LNAI-1221

## People

The development and application of agent technology has attracted some of
the brightest and the best in the world. Rather than list all the sites and e-mail
addresses, we recommend that you visit the following site, which lists over
one hundred of the top minds and does an excellent job of providing this information.

PEOPLE PAGE
http://www.cl.cam.ac.uk/users/rwab1/ag-people.html


## AGENTS SOFTWARE VENDORS

The market for software agents is still very young and fractured. Currently we have identified five specific types of vendors:

> *Vendors that use agents to enhance the capabilities of their products or services:* Examples include Oracle, Bay Networks, Microsoft, search engines on the Internet such as Infoseek and the news filtering systems personal news pages, and so on.
>
> *Vendors that create development environments or sell agent languages:* Examples include General Magic, Sun Microsystems' Quest Technologies, and IBM.
>
> *Vendors involved in research and development and publishing efforts on agents:* Examples include Apple Computer, Logica, and Bellcore.
>
> *Vendors that include agent functionality in their products and services:* Examples include Edify, Charles River Analytics, COMSHARE, AND AT&T.
>
> *Vendors that provide services and training:* Examples include Andersen Consulting and IBM.

The market for vendors is very attractive, and we expect to see many more enter the marketplace as agents become more popular.

One factor is apparent. **No one vendor has a dominant position, and the market is wide open for commercialization.**

Also, we expect to see much more commercial development of research projects as vendors form association with universities and colleges. The centers of learning are the nucleus of the industry, and many products have emerged to drive the market to more success.

The following is a list of sample vendors:

| | |
|---|---|
| Agents, Inc. | Desktop Data |
| Andersen Consulting | Digital Equipment, Inc. |
| Apple Computer | Dun & Bradstreet |
| AT&T | Edify, Inc. |
| Bay Networks | ELF Technologies |
| Beyond, Inc. | First Virtual Holdings |
| Caere, Inc. | General Magic |
| Charles River Analytics | Guideware Corporation |
| COMshare | Hewlett Packard |

IBM, Inc.                                    Planning Sciences
J & T Associates                             Quasar Knowledge
Legent                                       Questech
Logica                                       Sharp
Lotus, Inc.                                  Siemens
Microsoft, Inc.                              Software Ventures
Microstrategy                                South Beach Software
No Hands Software                            Sterling Software, Inc.
Olivetti                                     SunSoft
Oracle                                       Unisys
Ousterhout                                   Verity, Inc.
Personal Library Software, Inc.              Xpress

# 7

# What Are the Issues and Standards?

*. . . And trust no agent.*

—William Shakespeare, *Much Ado About Nothing*

The Internet is emerging as a global marketplace. The **legal framework supporting commercial transactions on the Internet should be governed by consistent principles across state, national, and international borders that lead to predictable results regardless of the jurisdiction in which a particular buyer or seller resides.**

We make no apology for the following excerpt from the U.S. Governments key statement on this area. It defines many of the critical issues facing the growth of the Internet and electronic commerce (a key user of agents). Our highlights, which we will address in this section, are in bold:-

### A Framework For Global Electronic Commerce

**President William J. Clinton**
**Vice President Albert Gore, Jr.**
**Washington, D.C.**

*"We are on the verge of a revolution that is just as profound as the change in the economy that came with the industrial revolution. Soon electronic networks will allow people to transcend the barriers of time and distance and take advantage of global markets and business opportunities not even imaginable today, opening up a new world of economic possibility and progress."*

*Vice President Albert Gore, Jr.*

Internet technology is having a profound effect on the global trade in services. World trade involving computer software, entertainment products (motion pictures, videos, games, sound recordings), information services (databases, online newspapers), technical information, product licenses, financial services, and professional services (businesses and technical consulting, accounting, architectural design, legal advice, travel services, etc.) has grown rapidly in the past decade, now accounting for well over $40 billion of U.S. exports alone.

SECTION II. Legal Issues

ITEM 3. 'UNIFORM COMMERICAL CODE' FOR ELECTRONIC COMMERCE

In general, parties should be able to do business with each other on the Internet under whatever terms and conditions they agree upon.

Private enterprise and free markets have typically flourished, however, where there are predictable and widely accepted legal environments supporting commercial transactions. To encourage electronic commerce, **the U.S. government should support the development of both a domestic and global uniform commercial legal framework that recognizes, facilitates, and enforces electronic transactions worldwide.** Fully informed buyers and sellers could voluntarily agree to form a contract subject to this uniform legal framework, just as parties currently choose the body of law that will be used to interpret their contract.

Participants in the marketplace should define and articulate most of the rules that will govern electronic commerce. To enable private entities to perform this task and to fulfill their roles adequately, governments should encourage the development of simple and predictable domestic and international rules and norms that will serve as the legal foundation for commercial activities in cyberspace.

In the United States, every state government has adopted the Uniform Commercial Code (UCC), a codification of substantial portions of commercial law. The National Conference of Commissioners of Uniform State Law (NCCUSL) and the **American Law Institute, domestic sponsors of the UCC, already are working to adapt the UCC to cyberspace.** Private sector organizations, including the American Bar Association (ABA) along with other interest groups, are participants in this process. Work is also ongoing on a proposed electronic contracting and records act for transactions not covered by the UCC. The Administration supports the prompt consideration of these proposals, and the adoption of uniform legislation by all states. Of course, any such legislation will be designed to accommodate ongoing and possible future global initiatives.

**Internationally, the United Nations Commission on International Trade Law (UNCITRAL) has completed work on a model law that supports the commercial use of international contracts in electronic commerce.** This model law establishes rules and norms that validate and recognize contracts formed through electronic means, sets default rules for contract formation and governance of electronic contract performance, defines the characteristics of a valid electronic writing and an original document, provides for the acceptability of electronic signatures for legal and commercial purposes, and supports the admission of computer evidence in courts and arbitration proceedings.

The United States Government supports the adoption of principles along these lines by all nations as a start to defining an international set of uniform commercial principles for electronic commerce. We urge UNCITRAL, other appropriate international bodies, bar associations, and other private sector groups to continue their work in this area.

The following principles should, to the extent possible, guide the drafting of rules governing global electronic commerce:

Parties should be free to order the contractual relationship between themselves as they see fit; rules should be technology-neutral (i.e., the rules should neither require nor assume a particular technology) and forward looking (i.e., the rules should not hinder the use or development of technologies in the future); existing rules should be modified and new rules should be adopted only as necessary or substantially desirable to support the use of electronic technologies; and the process should involve the high-tech commercial sector as well as businesses that have not yet moved online.

With these principles in mind, UNCITRAL, UNIDROIT, and the International Chamber of Commerce (ICC), and others should develop additional model provisions and uniform fundamental principles designed to eliminate administrative and regulatory barriers and to facilitate electronic commerce by:

encouraging governmental recognition, acceptance and facilitation of electronic communications (i.e., contracts, notarized documents, etc.); encouraging consistent international rules to support the acceptance of electronic signatures and other authentication procedures; and promoting the development of adequate, efficient, and effective alternate dispute resolution mechanisms for global commercial transactions.

The expansion of global electronic commerce also depends upon the participants' ability to **achieve a reasonable degree of certainty regarding their exposure to liability for any damage or injury that might result from their actions.** Inconsistent local tort laws, coupled with uncertainties regarding jurisdiction, could substantially increase litigation and create unnecessary costs that ultimately will be borne by consumers. The U.S. should work closely with other nations to clarify applicable jurisdictional rules and to generally favor and enforce contract provisions that allow parties to select substantive rules governing liability.

Finally, the development of global electronic commerce provides an opportunity to create legal rules that allow business and consumers to take advantage of new technology to streamline and automate functions now accomplished manually. For example, consideration should be given to establishing electronic registries.

The Departments of Commerce and State will continue to organize U.S. participation in these areas with a goal of achieving substantive international agreement on model law within the next two years. NCCUSL and the American Law Institute, working with the American Bar Association and other interested groups, are urged to continue their work to develop complementary domestic and international efforts.

**Standards are critical to the long term commercial success of the Internet** as they can allow products and services from different vendors to work together. They also encourage competition and reduce uncertainty in the global marketplace. Premature standardization, however, can "lock in" outdated technology. Standards also can be employed as de facto non-tariff trade barriers, to "lock out" non-indigenous businesses from a particular national market.

The United States believes that the marketplace, not governments, should determine technical standards and other mechanisms for interoperability. **Technology is moving rapidly and government attempts to establish technical standards to govern the Internet would only risk inhibiting technological innovation.** The United States considers it unwise and unnecessary for governments to mandate standards for electronic commerce. Rather, we urge industry driven multilateral fora to consider technical standards in this area. To ensure the growth of global electronic commerce over the Internet, standards will be needed to assure reliability, interoperability, ease of use and scalability in areas such as:

> electronic payments;
> security (confidentiality, authentication, data integrity, access control, non-repudiation);
> security services infrastructure (e.g., public key certificate authorities);
> electronic copyright management systems;
> video and data-conferencing;
> high-speed network technologies (e.g., Asynchronous Transfer Mode, Synchronous Digital Hierarchy); and
> digital object and data interchange.

There need not be one standard for every product or service associated with the GII , and technical standards need not be mandated. In some cases, multiple standards will compete for marketplace acceptance. In other cases, different standards will be used in different circumstances.

The prevalence of voluntary standards on the Internet, and the medium's consensus-based process of standards development and acceptance are stimulating its rapid growth. These standards flourish because of a non-bureaucratic system of development managed by technical practitioners working through various organizations. These organizations require demonstrated deployment of systems incorporating a given standard prior to formal acceptance, but the process facilitates rapid deployment of standards and can accommodate evolving standards as well. Only a handful of countries allow private sector standards development; most rely on governmental-mandated solutions, causing these nations to fall behind the technological cutting edge and creating non-tariff trade barriers.

Numerous private sector bodies have contributed to the process of developing voluntary standards that promote interoperability. The United States has encouraged the development of voluntary standards through private standards organizations, consortia, testbeds and R&D activities. (Examples include government support for 6bone, an IPv6 testbed; DARPA's support for CommerceNet, **the World Wide Web Consortium,** and research on multicast and quality of service; NSF's support for the Lightweight Directory Access

Protocol; and NIST's development of tools for testing compliance with the Virtual Reality Modeling Language [VRML] standard.)

The U.S. government also has adopted a set of principles to promote acceptance of domestic and international voluntary standards.

While no formal government-sponsored negotiations are called for at this time, the United States will use various fora (i.e., international alliances of private businesses, the International Organization for Standardization [ISO], the International Electrotechnical Commission [IEC], International Telecommunications Union [ITU], etc.) to discourage the use of standards to erect barriers to free trade on the developing GII. The private sector should assert global leadership to address standards setting needs. The United States will work through intergovernmental organizations as needed to monitor and support private sector leadership.

## THE WORLD OF STANDARDS—THE AGENCIES

Standards are so important in the area of Computer agents because once an agent starts to search through external material or to try to talk to servers or other agents, it requires considerable knowledge in common with them. It is useless for an agent to try to find the cheapest car on the market if each web server advertising cars for sale uses different protocols and formats to display or hold the pricing information. This situation would mean that the agent would have to understand and adapt to each different format or protocol, and doing that would make agents extremely unwieldly.

The existing standard for such information exchange is buried in native HTML and is extremely limited. The use of cookies allows a server to know what choices an individual may have made and to gain very primitive information about the browser being used for access. This limited information will be of little use in a more sophisticated world. The reason that clever shopping agents have not developed further than "Roboshopper" is that they have to be programmed for each site.

The following standards are all significant for various aspects of the Internet:

LDAP, MPLS, IPV6 6bone, OSD, CDF, CSS, DSSSL, XML, IITOP, COM, DCOM, CORBA, HTML, DHTML, KQML, p3p, Open Profiling, Content and Exchange, Metadata, RDF, EDI, EDIFACT, DOM

Unfortunately, even "standards" are not really standards unless **they are adopted by a wide enough range of suppliers and then corporate bodies to be meaningful.**

This drawback became very clear in the United Kingdom in the 1980s when the governments of all the world were saying that ISO is **the** standard for networks; many companies fell into the trap of believing this and spent huge sums of money to support ISO. Of course, history shows that TCP/IP became the de facto world standard for a number of reasons, mostly pragmatic and concerning practical working and speed. (ISO was so overdeveloped, it was too slow.) There was also a dearth of ISO software that companies who wished to "comply" were unable to do so.

In the Internet world, there are a number of bodies claiming to be defining standards and also, of course, significant commercial organizations—principally Microsoft, Sun, and Netscape—that are developing their own standards.

There are major world and U.S. standards bodies such as ANSII and ISO, but the Internet has moved so quickly that they have been effectively bypassed. Therefore, we must examine the "standards" existing and emerging in the light of this complexity. The main bodies working in the areas that affect computer agents are as follows:

> **Worldwide Web Consortium W3C:** The preceding U.S. government quote acknowledges this body uniquely as being one that it considers significant. It is also interesting to note that virtually all recognized standards **in use** on the Web are from this body. We would go so far as to state that if WWW does not approve, things don't happen.
>
> **ARPA:** Although mentioned in the same quote, ARPA is a government agency, and the quote specifically says that the U.S. government prefers **not** to use government agencies. ARPA will continue to lead the Internet through research and new developments (such as Internet2), but it is WWW and IETF that will control introduction.
>
> **Open Group:** This body was set up prior to the emergence of the Internet as the main future of all networks and systems. It was set up to promote "open" standards for objects or agents to use for communication and access to information. Most of the key developers seem to be subscribing to the basic tenets of Object communication such as Object Request Brokering.
>
> **Internet Engineering Task Force (IETF):** This group is very influential for the basic design and architecture of the underlying network. Of course, this is significant in regard to agents in that efficient routing and flow will affect the ability of agents to function with certain tasks.
>
> **FIPA:** This is a recent group formed to coordinate work on agents. It is unclear whether it will have any impact. Currently no FIPA protocol or language is being used.

And here are the commercial giants:

> **Sun**
> Most significant for the Java language
>
> **Netscape**
> Generally supporting Java standards

**Microsoft**
Promoting Active X technology
**IBM**
Promoting Aglets and Java

## THE WORLD OF STANDARDS—THE STANDARDS TODAY
## AND PROPOSED STANDARDS

The following is a description of standards bodies who is involved and their background.

## THE OPEN GROUP

Their mission: To cause the creation of a viable, global, information infrastructure that is ubiquitous, trusted, reliable, and as easy to use as the telephone.

### IT Dialtone

The IT dialtone is applicable to enterprises, small businesses, and consumers. It provides for exchange of value between Information Service Users in the broadest sense. It must be able to provide support for enterprises for their internal communication, for business partnership interactions between separate businesses, and for the support of consumer systems, all on the same network and at the same time. The IT Dialtone is a single standard information infrastructure suitable for, and available to, all. It must therefore provide a common public information infrastructure that has a quality of service, in terms of performance, security, reliability, and scaleability appropriate to its use as a primary means of business interaction; and it must have the capability to support a broad range of compelling service-offerings that will stimulate widespread consumer use.

## THE WORLD WIDE WEB CONSORTIUM (W3C)

The W3C was created to develop common protocols that enhance the interoperability and promote the evolution of the World Wide Web. It is an industry consortium jointly run by the MIT Laboratory for Computer Science (LCS) in the United States, the National Institute for Research in Computer Science and Control (INRIA) in France, and Keio University in Japan. Services provided by the Consortium include a repository of information about the World Wide Web for developers and users; sample code implementations to embody and promote standards; and various prototype and sample applications to demonstrate the use of new technology. To date, more than 250 organizations are members of the Consortium.

## P3P

In October 1997, the World Wide Web Consortium (W3C) announced the first public results from the Platform for Privacy Preferences Project (P3P), which helps ensure that users' privacy concerns are respected on the Web.

Two working drafts, Architectural Overview, and Grammatical Model, are the result of the initial P3P working groups. Key industry players, including Art Technology Group, AT&T Labs, Bellcore, Center for Democracy and Technology, Digital Equipment Corp., DCOMPUTER AGENTS, DoubleClick, Engage Technologies, Ernst & Young LLP, Firefly Network, IBM, Intermind Corp., MatchLogic, MCI Communications, Microsoft, MIT, Narrowline, NEC, Netscape Communications, Open Market, Open Sesame, Oracle Corp., Sony, The DMA, TRUSTe, U.C. Irvine, and VeriSign are participating in the W3C P3P Working Groups.

The term *privacy* covers a very wide range of concerns, and it is important to understand from the outset the precise scope of the P3P work. P3P will enable sites to express privacy practices and for users to express their preferences about those practices and to have their agent act on it accordingly. The user agent can then provide the user a safe and seamless experience.

A P3P interaction will result in an agreement between the service and the user agent regarding the practices associated with a user's implicit (that is, click stream) or explicit (that is, user-answered) data. The agreement may include service side permissions regarding the storage and release of data written by the service and accepted by the user agent. Allowing client side storage of user data in a data repository increases the user's access to and control of data, while providing a mechanism so that the user need not repeatedly enter frequently solicited information. This architecture enhances personal privacy while providing richer, easier access to Web services. The larger goal of P3P is to create a framework that promotes trust and confidence in the Web. We believe that the key ideas are the following:

The disclosure of site privacy practices.

The expression of a user's preferences with respect to which practices the user prefers.

The ability of the site and user agent to reach an agreement about their interactions with respect to data privacy.

Subsequent to an agreement, the controlled and secure exchange of data on behalf of the user to the service that defined or requested the data.

## WEB DESIGN STANDARDS

### SGML, an ISO Standard That Started It All

SGML, the Standard Generalized Markup Language, prescribes the rules for creating a specific markup language such as HTML. In other words, HTML is an application of SGML. HTML is a single set of tags, whereas SGML provides the capability for creating any desired set of tags. XML is similar to SGML in that it likewise provides the capability to create any tags. Unfortunately SGML did not lend itself to the simple creation of Web pages that led to HTML.

### HTML

HTML is popular for a number of reasons:

*It is very simple:* HTML makes Web cruising so simple that most people can train themselves. All you have to learn is how to click on the blue underlined text. For those who want to create simple Web pages, HTML is easy enough to learn in just a few hours.

*It has built-in style:* The screen formatting that is built into HTML is likewise very simple. Even though HTML formatting has a lot of limitations, it's far better than the plain text display of the Internet before the advent of HTML and the World Wide Web. HTML's limited formatting options make Web publishing even easier, because you don't have to deal with balancing multiple columns, positioning graphics to achieve attractive page breaks, and so on.

*It has easy, standard linking:* HTML's flexible and powerful hypertext linking is easy to set up, but it, too, has limitations that complicate large-scale implementations.

*It has forms support:* You can easily set up simple forms applications with HTML. Today's Web editors make it possible for you to set up your first form in an hour or two. After you've done your first form, you can do additional forms in much less time.

*It has simple programming:* Finally, HTML uses CGI scripting for really easy programming. Although you can't do everything with it, you can do a decent amount really easily.

However, HTML is now proving a barrier to the delivery of a higher level of information and service. It is just too simple and cannot specify information properly for negotiation. There are two choices—move to SGML where it all began, or look at an expansion of the HTML features.

SGML has not proved popular. In can be compared with the situation in the 1980s with the ISO networking standards. It is so comprehensive and flexible that it is hard to define well enough for two groups to write code that is still exchangeable! It is cumbersome (as were ISO network standards) and code heavy. To overcome this problem, the W3C has proposed XML, which follows.

## XML

During the course of our writing this book, the W3C has accepted XML as the next generation of HTML (April 17, 1998). This endorsement will accelerate the work in this area as follows.

XML, or Extensible Markup Language, is a highly functional subset of SGML. The purpose of XML is to specify an SGML subset that works very well for delivering SGML information over the Web. When the mainstream Web browsers support XML, we believe that it's going to be very easy to publish SGML information on the Web.

### Why Is a New Language Required?

HTML has a lot going for it, but HTML also has several limitations that become apparent for applications that are larger or more functional than home pages and small Web sites. The following paragraphs explain these limitations in detail.

*Limited Structure.*   Most of HTML's limitations can be traced to its fixed set of tags, which primarily serve to specify formatting of documents delivered on the Web. In other words, HTML tags support only a fixed and trivially simple structure.

HTML's lack of structure creates significant barriers to using HTML for applications beyond simple browsing, such as reuse, interchange, and automation. Each of these is covered in the following paragraphs.

*Limited Reuse.*   Many organizations publish the same information in multiple forms; it's very common to have both printed and Web forms of the same data. Information originally created in HTML can be reused for printing, and information originally created for printing can be reused for Web delivery. However, to achieve reuse requires conversion that's usually followed by manual intervention to fix up the appearance (that is, the formatting) of the resulting document. And that means that each time the source information changes, the conversion and fix-up process must be repeated. Because this is an expensive, time-consuming, and labor-intensive process, organizations with lots of data to distribute have preferred to adopt SGML.

*Limited Interchange.*   Because the Internet is simple and ubiquitous, it provides an ideal medium for organizations that want to interchange data. However, HTML undermines interchange because its small, fixed set of tags primarily indicates only the appearance of an element of a document. HTML provides nothing to denote the data within a document, thus crippling attempts to achieve reuse.

*For example, a computer manufacturer may wish to capture semiconductor data from its suppliers and feed that data into its computer-aided design (CAD) systems. Its CAD systems require data such as the function, tolerances, and timing of each pin of an integrated circuit. HTML provides no way to tag such data unambiguously. In fact, even if the original source data contains the necessary tagging to eliminate uncertainty, which is likely to be the case if the source data is in SGML, the resulting down-translation to HTML strips all the intelligence away.*

*Limited Automation.*    Automation saves labor, reduces costs, speeds delivery, and improves quality. There are many opportunities for adding automation to the use of the Web, particularly for Intranets and Extranets. Examples include almost any forms-based application, such as insurance enrollments, medical claims processing, and online banking.

However, HTML poses a significant barrier to achieving automation. All highly automated processes are built on a data format that's highly expressive and absolutely consistent. HTML lacks the necessary expressiveness, since it's limited to a fixed set of presentation-oriented tags, and also lacks the absolute consistency, since there's no way to impose a rigorous data structure on top of those tags.

To move forward and eliminate some of these problems, XML is being promoted by the W3C. XML is almost indistinguishable from SGML as practiced. XML has almost all of the capabilities of SGML that are widely supported. XML lacks only some important capabilities of SGML that primarily affect document creation, not document delivery.

XML is the Extensible Markup Language subset of ISO's Standard Generalized Markup Language (SGML) developed by the World Wide Web Consortium (W3C) "SGML on the Web" working party during the latter half of 1996 and early 1997. The formal recommendation was submitted for approval by W3C members on December 8, 1997.

### XML's Inventors

XML is being designed by a Working Group of the World Wide Web Consortium (W3C), an organization whose charter is to establish specifications for Web technologies to ensure the highest possible degree of utility and interoperability.

The XML Working Group consists of about fourteen companies and organizations with a strong interest in either providing or utilizing XML tools. This group includes Adobe, ArborText, DataChannel, Fuji, Xerox, Hewlett-Packard, Inso, Isogen, Microsoft, Netscape, SoftQuad, Sun Microsystems, and the University of Chicago, along with Dan Connolly, a W3C representative, and James Clark, an independent expert. Most of the Working Group members bring considerable experience with SGML to the task of defining and refining XML.

### The Growing Momentum Behind XML

Momentum behind XML has grown at a startling rate since development of the XML specification began in September 1996:

- Microsoft has already shipped XML support in Internet Explorer 4.0, and they're likely to expand their XML functionality even further in the next release. Netscape will potentially support XML in the 1998 version of Navigator.
- Many other companies have already announced or will soon announce XML support in their products. It's very likely that all of the companies represented in the XML Working Group will either support or utilize XML within the next year.
- Articles about XML frequently appear in mainstream IT publications such as *InfoWorld* and *PC Week*, and XML is receiving extensive coverage by influential newsletters such as *Seybold Reports*.
- Major industry analyst services such as Gartner Group, Meta Group, and CAP Ventures are covering XML, sometimes from a Web publishing view and other times from a print publishing view.

By now, it's become evident that XML will become the primary means to deliver over the Web the vast amount of SGML-based information that currently exists. In fact, XML is likely to become the underlying technology for powering Intranets and Extranets, which leverage the power of the Internet for serious business applications.

## XML/EDI

An interesting development based on XML has been the definition of an XML/EDI standard to promote commerce.

Electronic data interchange has been in use for a quarter century. Despite the long history and numerous advantages of EDI, only an estimated 125,000 organizations worldwide have an EDI system. Furthermore, there are only 80,000 EDI-enabled businesses in the United States. That number works out to less than 2 percent of the 6.2 million businesses registered in the United States. Because of the cost and complexity, small and medium-sized businesses find it difficult to implement and maintain a traditional EDI system. For these reasons, most businesses do not enjoy the operating efficiencies that an automated electronic information routing system proposes. (See the accompanying figure "EDI Today.") The obstacles that businesses must overcome to start their EDI/EC implementation seem insurmountable, but that situation is changing with the advent of XML/EDI.

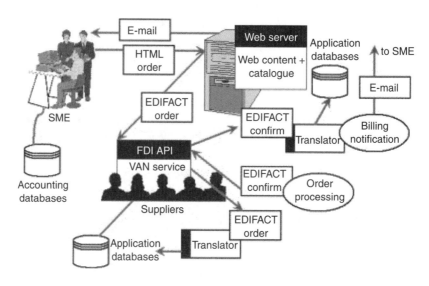

**EDI Today**

On September 10, 1997, a proposal for a new form of XML Style Language (XSL), which incorporates the ECMAScript standardized variant of JavaScript, was published by a consortium led by Microsoft, ArborText, and Inso Corp. This version of the XML/EDI specification uses the power provided by this new advanced language combination to show how control of XML/EDI document processes can be achieved in a distributed manner.

In October 1997, a specification for a formal Document Object Model (DOM) for XML documents was published by W3C. This model provides a standardized API for XML-based tools. Combining XML and EDI to develop XML/EDI suggests that the main method of capturing and coding EDI information will be through XML-coded electronic forms. At present, the form-handling characteristics of XML are yet to be fully agreed on (agreement is expected during 1998). To allow interaction with existing systems, the XML/EDI Guidelines show how EDIFACT messages can be generated from XML/EDI forms, and vice versa. (See the accompanying figure.)

Unfortunately, not all in the garden is rosy. Another group is proposing an alternative EDI/Internet standard known as ICE.

## Information & Content Exchange (ICE) Protocol

Firefly Network, Inc., Vignette Corp., and other Internet commerce companies have launched an effort to create a standard means for exchanging data that will allow merchants and their suppliers more easily to design online superstores.

The Web software and service companies, which also include Adobe Systems, Inc. (ADBE), CNet, Inc. (CNWK), the JavaSoft division of Sun Microsys-

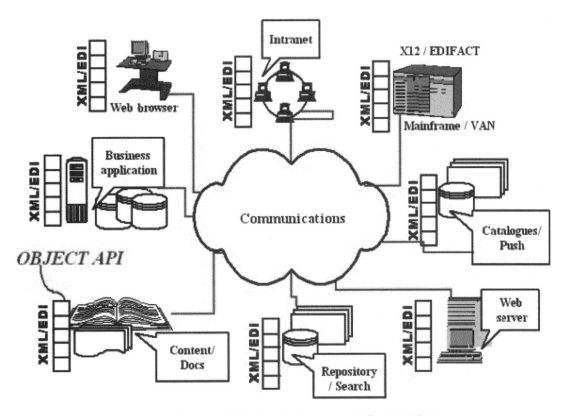

**Proposed Electronic Commerce Using XML/EDI**

tems, Inc. (SUN), Tribune Media Services, and Ziff-Davis, Inc., intend to establish a set of technical specifications that will allow information on products and prices to be exchanged easily between Web servers.

The Information & Content Exchange (ICE) Protocol would be based on the Extensible Markup Language, a "meta" language that is designed to make it easier to organize data by keeping track of information included in Web documents. It would also comply with the Open Profiling Standard that would convey only that data about customers that they have approved of disseminating.

The ICE standard, if adopted widely, would allow merchandise, service, or information retailers to draw quickly on data that resides on hundreds of suppliers' servers. An online travel megasite would be easier to construct, since that site operator could receive constantly updated information on restaurants, hotels, vacation packages, local events, and the like, without worrying about incompatible forms of data.

"This is EDI [electronic document interchange] for the Internet," said Ross Garber, Vignette's chief executive. "It is harnessing the power of the supply chain."

The ICE Protocol also would help superstore operators and their vendors to encode rules about how they want to do business with each other, in an automated fashion.

### XSL: Stylesheets

*Based on DSSSL.* After SGML became an international standard, work began on developing a stylesheet standard. The purpose of the standard was to facilitate the interchange of stylesheets and ultimately to improve the interoperability of all of the software that handles documents. This effort, formally known as the Document Style Semantics and Specification Language (DSSSL), was eventually approved as an ISO standard. To date, however, no commercial application supports DSSSL. XSL will provide much of the functionality of DSSSL, but in a form that is far more likely to be widely adopted and supported.

*Compatible with CSS.* Cascading Style Sheets (CSS) are supported by both Microsoft and Netscape as a mechanism for overriding the default style of HTML tags. As a result, CSS offers more formatting flexibility than HTML without a stylesheet. XSL will be a superset of the CSS functionality. XSL will be designed to enable automatic conversion from CSS, so existing investments in CSS will not be lost.

*Reordering Capability.* Through XSL stylesheets, a Web browser will be able to change the sequence of the data that is displayed without going back to the server. This ability will be useful for any application that needs to support the interactive suppression or enabling of data display, as well as any arbitrary sequence.

*More Powerful Context Sensitivity.* Whereas CSS supports the application of style on the basis of the parent of an element, XSL allows the style to vary on the basis of all the ancestors, descendants, and siblings of an element. This ability will provide far more formatting flexibility based on the context or position of an element within a document.

*Supports Both Printing and Online Display.* Whereas CSS is limited to online display functions, XSL will support formatting functions that are needed in order to support the greater complexity of printed documents.

### XLL: Superior Linking for XML

*Takes Advantage of HyTime and TEI.* XLL will be designed to take advantage of the linking concepts in HyTime and the Text Encoding Initiative (TEI). Although these standards have not been widely implemented by software vendors, they provide several powerful improvements to standard HTML linking as well as other features outside the scope of XLL.

*Compatible with Existing URL Linking.*    XLL will fully support the existing link formats of the Web.

*Bi-directional Links.*    Bi-directional links will allow the user to initiate a traversal from either direction of two pieces of information that are linked together.

*Addressing.*    XLL will allow links to pinpoint a certain hierarchical location within a target XML document.

*Indirect Links.*    Indirect links will vastly improve the maintainability of large collections of Web documents. Currently, if the target of a link changes its path, the file containing the source link must be changed as well. Consider the simple case in which a Seattle Web site points to a page on a Detroit Web site. If the location of that Detroit page changes, then the link on the Seattle Web site must be changed too. Permissions for making those changes are likely to be different, so two individuals must manually interact and coordinate. For complex webs, the result can be a nightmare involving high costs and frustrated users. Indirect links solve that problem. Through XLL, linking will occur indirectly, through a separate, intermediate link file. When a file changes location, only the intermediate file needs to be changed; the source file and destination files can remain intact.

## Metadata

One of the differences between SGML and XML is the DTD, a separate protocol for data handling. In XML this is replaced with inline coding known as RDF.

RDF—the Resource Description Framework—is a foundation for processing metadata; it provides interoperability between applications that exchange machine-understandable information on the Web. RDF emphasizes facilities to enable automated processing of Web resources. RDF metadata can be used in a variety of application areas; for example, in resource discovery to provide better search engine capabilities; in cataloging for describing the content and content relationships available at a particular Web site, page, or digital library; by computer agents to facilitate knowledge sharing and exchange; in content rating; in describing collections of pages that represent a single logical "document"; for describing intellectual property rights of Web pages; and in many others. RDF with digital signatures will be key to building the "Web of Trust" for electronic commerce, collaboration, and other applications.

Metadata is "data about data," or specifically in the context of RDF, "data describing Web resources." The distinction between "data" and "metadata" is not an absolute one; it is a distinction created primarily by a particular application. Many times the same resource will be interpreted in both ways simultaneously. RDF encourages this view by using XML as the encoding syntax for the metadata. The resources being described by RDF are, in general, anything that can be named via a URL. The broad goal of RDF is to define a mechanism for describing resources that makes no assumptions about a particular application domain, nor defines the semantics of any application domain. The definition of the mechanism should be domain neutral, yet the mechanism should be suitable for describing information about any domain.

## PICS (Platform for Internet Content Selection)

PICS defines a language for describing rating services. Software programs will read service descriptions written in this language, in order to interpret content labels and assist end-users in configuring selection software. A related document (PICS Label Distribution) specifies the syntax and semantics of content labels and protocol(s) for distributing labels.

The goal of the PICS effort is to enable a marketplace in which many different products and services will be developed, tested, and compared. Hence, the following considerations have had significant impact on this document:

- Some organizations may rate items on well-known dimensions, using their own techniques and viewpoints to determine actual ratings. Other organizations may choose to develop their own dimensions for rating. This preference motivates the distinction between a rating system and a rating service.
- Some services may provide access to their ratings online, from an HTTP server, while others may either ship them in batches or transmit them on floppy disks or CD-ROMs.

What is a "rating service"? A rating service is an individual, group, organization, or company that provides content labels for information on the Internet. The labels it provides are based on a rating system (see later). Each rating service must describe itself using a newly created MIME type, application/pics-service. Selection software that relies on ratings from a PICS rating service can first load the application/pics-service description. This description allows the software to tailor its user interface to reflect the details of a particular rating service, rather than providing a "one design fits all rating services" interface.

This specification does not state how the application/pics-service description of a rating service is initially located. For users of the World Wide Web, we expect that well-known sites will provide lists of rating services along with their application/pics-service descriptions. It is expected that client programs will cache copies of application/pics-service descriptions, so any incompatible change in a service description should be accomplished by creating an entirely new service URL.

Each rating service picks a URL as its unique identifier, which is included in all content labels that the service produces, to identify their source. We recommend, but do not require, that this identifier include a version number, as shown in all of the examples in this specification, to simplify transitions due to incompatible changes over time. For example, our sample service "http://www.gcf.org/v1.0/" includes "v1.0" as its own version number. To ensure that no other service uses the same identifier, it must be a valid URL. In addition, the URL (when used within a query) serves as a default location for a label bureau that dispenses this service's labels (see the information on PICS Label Distribution earlier in this section).

What is a "rating system"? A rating system specifies the dimensions used for labeling, the scale of allowable values on each dimension, and a description of the criteria used in assigning values. For example, the MPAA rates movies in the United States on the basis of a single dimension with allowable values G, PG, PG-13, R, and NC-17.

Each rating system is identified by a valid URL. This identification enables several services to use the same rating system and refer to it by its identifier. The URL naming a rating system can be accessed to obtain a human-readable description of the rating system. The format of that description is not specified.

## ARPA—THE KNOWLEDGE SHARING EFFORT

The ARPA Knowledge Sharing Effort (KSE) is a consortium to develop conventions facilitating the sharing and reuse of knowledge bases and knowledge-based systems. Its goal is to define, develop, and test infrastructure and supporting technology to enable participants to build much bigger and more broadly functional systems than could be achieved working alone.

Current approaches for building knowledge-based systems usually involve constructing new knowledge bases from scratch. The ability to efficiently scale up AI technology will require the sharing and reuse of existing components. This requirement is equally true of software modules as well as conceptual knowledge. AI system developers could then focus on the creation of the specialized knowledge and reasoners new to the task at hand. New systems could interoperate with existing systems, using them to perform some of its reasoning. In this way, declarative knowledge, problem solving techniques, and reasoning services could all be shared among systems. The ability to build, manage and use sharable and reusable knowledge resources is thought to be a key to the realization of large-scale intelligent systems. The definition of conventions enabling sharing among collaborators is the essential first step toward these goals.

The KSE is organized around four working groups, each of which is addressing a complementary problem identified in current knowledge representation technology:

- The Interlingua Group is concerned with translation between different representation languages, with subinterests in translation at design time and at run-time.

- The KRSS Group (Knowledge Representation System Specification) is concerned with defining common constructs within families of representation languages.
- The SRKB Group (Shared, Reusable Knowledge Bases) is concerned with facilitating consensus on the contents of sharable knowledge bases, with subinterests in shared knowledge for particular topic areas and in topic-independent development tools/methodologies.
- The External Interfaces Group is concerned with run-time interactions between knowledge-based systems and other modules in a run-time environment, with subinterests in communication protocols for KB-to-KB and for KB-to-DB.

The KQML language is one of the main results that have come out of the external interfaces group of the KSE.

## KQML—A Language and Protocol for Knowledge and Information Exchange

Knowledge Query and Manipulation Language (KQML) is a new language and protocol for exchanging information and knowledge. This work is part of a larger effort, the ARPA Knowledge Sharing Effort, which is aimed at developing techniques and a methodology for building large-scale knowledge bases that are sharable and reusable.

KQML is both a message format and a message-handling protocol to support run-time knowledge sharing among agents. KQML can be used as a language for an application program to interact with an intelligent system or for two or more intelligent systems to share knowledge in support of cooperative problem solving.

Many computer systems are structured as collections of independent processes—these are frequently distributed across multiple hosts linked by a network. Database processes, real-time processes, and distributed AI systems are a few examples. Furthermore, in modern network systems, it should be possible to build new programs by extending existing systems; a new small process should be conveniently linkable to existing information sources and tools (such as filters or rule based systems).

The idea of an architecture where this process is easy to do is quite appealing. (It is regularly mentioned in science fiction.) Many proposals for intelligent user-agents such as Knowbots (Kahn) assume the existence of this type of environment. One type of program that would thrive in such an environment is a mediator (Wiederhold). Mediators are processes that situate themselves between provider processes and consumer processes and perform services on the raw information such as providing standardized interfaces; integrating information from several sources; and translating queries or replies. Mediators (also known as middleware) are becoming increasingly important because they are commonly proposed as an effective method for integrating new information systems with inflexible legacy systems.

However, networks environments that support "plug and play" processes are still rare, and most distributed systems are implemented with ad hoc interfaces between their components. Many Internet resources, such as library catalog access, finger, and menu based systems, are designed to support only process-to-user interaction. Those which support process-to-process communication, such as ftp or the Mosaic World Wide Web browser, rely on fairly primitive communication protocols.

The reason for this situation is that there are no adequate standards to support complex communication among processes. Existing protocols, such as RPC, are insufficient for several reasons. They are not all that standard; there are currently several successful and incompatible RPC standards (for example, ONC and DCE). They are also too low level; they do not provide high-level access to information, but are intended only as "remote procedure calls."

Nor are there standard models for programming in an environment where some of the data is supplied by processes running on remote machines and some of the results are needed by other similarly distant processes. Although there are many ad hoc techniques for accomplishing what is needed, it is important that standard methods be adopted as early as is reasonable in order to facilitate and encourage the use of these new architectures. It is not enough for it to be possible to communicate; it must be easy to communicate. Not only should low-level communication tasks such as error checking be automatic, but using and observing protocol should be automatic as well.

KQML is a language and a protocol that supports this type of network programming specifically for knowledge-based systems or intelligent agents. It was developed by the ARPA supported Knowledge Sharing Effort (Neches 91, Patil 92) and separately implemented by several research groups. It has been successfully used to implement a variety of information systems using different software architectures.

## FIPA

The Foundation for Intelligent Physical Agents (FIPA) is a nonprofit association registered in Geneva, Switzerland. FIPA's purpose is to promote the success of emerging agent-based applications, services, and equipment. This goal is pursued by making available in a timely manner, internationally agreed-upon specifications that maximise inter-operability across agent-based applications, services, and equipment. This goal is realised through the open international collaboration of member organizations which are companies and universities active in the agent field. FIPA intends to make the results of its activities available to all interested parties and to contribute the results of its activities to appropriate formal standards bodies.

This specification has been developed through direct involvement of the FIPA membership. The thirty-five corporate members of FIPA (October 1997) represent twelve countries from all over the world.

Membership in FIPA is open to any corporation and individual firm, partnership, governmental body, or international organization without restriction. By joining FIPA, each member declares herself or himself individually and collectively committed to open competition in the development of agent-based applications, services, and equipment. Associate member status is usually chosen by those entities who do want to be members of FIPA without using the right to influence the precise content of the specifications through voting.

The members are not restricted in any way from designing, developing, marketing, and/or procuring agent-based applications, services, and equipment. Members are not bound to implement or use specific agent-based standards, recommendations, and FIPA specifications by virtue of their participation in FIPA.

This specification is published as FIPA 97 ver. 1.0 after two previous versions have been subject to public comments following disclosure on the WWW. It has undergone intense review by members as well non-members. FIPA is now starting a validation phase by encouraging its members to carry out field trials that are based on this specification. During 1998 FIPA will publish FIPA 97 ver. 2.0 that will incorporate whatever adaptations will be deemed necessary to take into account the results of field trials.

### Introduction

This FIPA 97 specification is the first output of the Foundation for Intelligent Physical Agents. It provides many different specifications of basic agent technologies that can be integrated by agent systems developers to make complex systems with a high degree of inter-operability.

FIPA specifies the interfaces of the different components in the environment with which an agent can interact, that is, humans, other agents, non-agent software, and the physical world. See the accompanying figure. FIPA produces the following two kinds of specification:

- **normative** specifications that mandate the external behavior of an agent and ensure inter-operability with other FIPA-specified subsystems; and
- **informative** specifications of applications for guidance to industry on the use of FIPA technologies.

The first set of specifications—called FIPA 97—has seven parts:

- three normative parts for basic agent technologies: agent management, agent communication language, and agent/software integration; and
- four informative application descriptions that provide examples of how the normative items can be applied: personal travel assistance, personal assis-

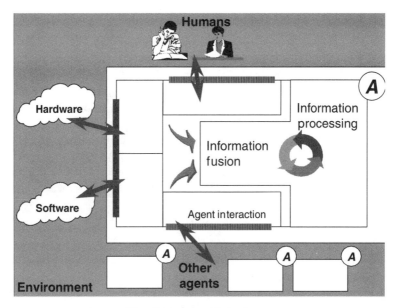

**The FIPA Agent Interfaces**

tant, audio-visual entertainment and broadcasting, and network management and provisioning.

Overall, the three FIPA 97 technologies allow

- the construction and management of an agent system composed of different agents, possibly built by different developers;
- agents to communicate and interact with each other to achieve individual or common goals; and
- legacy software or new nonagent software systems to be used by agents.

A brief illustration of FIPA 97 specification follows.

### Part 1—Agent Management

This part of FIPA 97 provides a normative framework within which FIPA compliant agents can exist, operate, and be managed. It defines an agent platform reference model containing such capabilities as white and yellow pages, message routing, and life-cycle management. True to the FIPA approach, these capabilities are themselves intelligent agents using formally sound communicative acts based on special message sets. An appropriate ontology and content language allows agents to discover each other's capabilities.

### Part 2—Agent Communication Language

The FIPA Agent Communication Language (ACL) is based on speech act theory: Messages are actions, or *communicative* acts, as they are intended to perform some action by virtue of being sent. The specification consists of a set of message types and the description of their pragmatics, that is, the effects on the mental attitudes of the sender and receiver agents. Every communicative act is described with both a normative form and a formal semantics based on modal logic.

The specifications include guidance to users who are already familiar with KQML in order to facilitate migration to the FIPA ACL. The specification also provides the normative description of a set of high-level interaction protocols, including requesting an action, contract net, and several kinds of auctions, and the like.

### Part 3—Agent/Software Integration

This part applies to any other nonagentized software with which agents need to "connect." Such software includes legacy software, conventional database systems, and middleware for all manners of interaction including hardware drivers. Because in most significant applications, nonagentized software may dominate software agents, Part 3 provides important normative statements. It suggests ways by which agents may connect to software via "wrappers" including specifications of the wrapper ontology and the software dynamic registration mechanism. For this purpose, an Agent Resource Broker (ARB) service is defined, which allows advertisement of nonagent services in the agent domain and management of their use by other agents, such as negotiation of parameters (for example, cost and priority), authentication, and permission.

## AGENT CRITICISMS

Not all the press articles, books, and other media have been positive about the potential of agent technology. Criticisms are numerous, loud, and everywhere. Examples include the following:

- Agents are not new but merely an extension of the work done in Artificial Intelligence (AI) research and development.
- Agents are not "Intelligent (there may be some truth in this statement, which we shall discuss this later in the book).
- Agents have been around for several years and have not taken off.
- Agents will not enhance or develop the potential of the Internet and other networks.
- The applications for agents are severely limited.
- Excessive searching using agents will cause response times problems on the Internet.

- Agents are overhyped and not applicable to the Internet.
- Agent technology will not prove beneficial and will fade away.

It is not our intention to address these weak arguments or to waste precious reading time debating the issues supplied here. We make only this one comment: **When we first encountered the Internet, a stuffy professor told us, "Don't waste your time with the World Wide Web concept; no one who understands the Internet will ever need such a silly tool."** With the introduction of a sophisticated technology, there are bound to be issues raised regarding its acceptance and use. Among the issues being debated at this time include the following:

*Hype:* There has been a good deal of hype over the past few years, including untruths and unrealistic expectations in the media, from vendors, and in the press. The main goal must be to reset expectations through education and realistic results. Agents will not take over the Web or the world.

*Security:* Safeguards are needed to guarantee system and data security while unknown agents are visiting or requesting information from various systems. Some users will not allow agents to roam their Web sites, and they expect a new industry to emerge that prevents agent entry. Security is a sensitive issue, particularly in the corporate world.

*Privacy:* Privacy, which is related to security, will be an issue. Some users want to gather the maximum amount of information and have their agents roam a large number of networks, while at the same time they are not eager to share their own information. Limits will be set for agent access.

*Performance:* As agents proliferate, they will require more computer time. This requirement could result in purportedly unobtrusive agents consuming the most power. If a large number of systems are using agents, internal network traffic problems are also at risk. Will there be an "agent surplus"?

*Legal issues:* Many legal issues will arise as agents that operate on an owner's behalf may request information, use that information, and make decisions that could be damaging to other users. If an agent makes a contested decision, it could be difficult to determine who is responsible. Clearly, legal precedents need to be set.

*Intelligence:* Agents will gain intelligence. Just what do we mean by intelligence? And how much control do we delegate to agents? Many social issues could arise here. If an agent corrects bad habits of its owners—who or what determines behavior?

*Owner expectations:* The use of agent related terminology and attributes associated with agents will produce unreasonable expectations and confusion. The signs of this outcome's happening are already evident.

## LEGAL ISSUES

---

### BMI Seeking to Get a Handle on Music on the Web

NEW YORK (AP) 15 October 1997—The music licensing agency BMI has developed a "Web robot" to monitor transmission and sales of music on the Internet, a possible precursor to messy copyright battles.

An estimated 26,000 Web sites use some form of music and only a handful have licensing agreements with BMI, the organization said Wednesday. BMI represents more than 180,000 songwriters and song publishers and is responsible for making sure they are compensated when their work is performed. In a simpler age, it meant keeping track of jukebox and radio play of songs.

Until development of its "Musicbot" system, the agency has been unable to get a grip on the explosion of outlets where people can buy, trade or simply listen to music on the Internet. Many people who use music on Web sites are simply unaware of copyright laws, said BMI president and CEO Frances Preston. "The sophisticated people who are doing the larger Web sites are certainly aware of the rights of intellectual property," she said. "They should come forward and secure the proper rights. But they don't."

BMI's invention works as a lightning-fast Web surfer to identify sites that use music and how often computer users visit them. It can potentially be used to keep track of the most popular music bought or transmitted on the Web, sort of a cyber top 10.

It also serves to put Web site designers on notice that BMI is watching. Although BMI has not started any legal proceedings against potential copyright violators on the Web, "it stands to reason in the future that it will happen," said Richard Conlon, a BMI vice president.

Teenagers who download a copy of the latest Nine Inch Nail song from a friend shouldn't worry too much. But services that sell large amounts of music may hear from BMI, said Joanne Marino, editor-in-chief of Webnoize, a music and media trade publication.

BMI officials are also in the midst of copyright discussions with record companies that disseminate music through Web sites. "Clearly, the trend is the music industry is evolving into an online entity, a more virtual marketplace," Marino said. "Anything that provides a way for the industry to become more educated" about the Internet is helpful, she said.

BMI doesn't see online music as a particularly fruitful source of revenue right now, but it wanted to be in a position to take advantage of it if the Web continues to grow exponentially as a music source, Conlon said.

As this example illustrates, there are legal implications of publishing on the Internet that have been difficult to define or act upon.

Agents play a part on both sides of the legal divide. In this case, an agent is working for the owner of the rights to music and is sweeping the Web to find illegal use. In other examples, it is the agent itself that while attempting to fulfill its destiny, transgresses the law.

Take, for example, an agent (perhaps sent by a newspaper reporter) that searches corporate databases for signs of illegal activity (such as waste dumping). If the agent was successful in its search but found the information in files that were not published directly but obtained it by following links, the legality of the discovery might well be questioned.

Some agents already transgress the boundary of what we think of as legal. When your browser accesses the Internet, it is passing on to each host which asks information about you. This information is made available through a kind of agent called a cookie. Cookies pass on all kinds of information about your computer, the operating system, and the browser itself.

---

Grace Hopper (the second programmer on the first computer in the world and the greatest lady in computing history) once said, "There are two great and opposing forces in the amendments to the U.S. Constitution, the Right to Privacy and the Freedom of Information Act." Her view was that these two amendments would clash at some future time, with dire consequences for the Constitution itself.

The Internet may be the battleground.

---

## LIABILITY

In law, the question of liability is affected by the question, Is computer programming a profession?

The issue of whether computer programming is a profession is important to the issue of software liability in this sense: Professionals are held to higher standards of duty when it comes to negligence determinations. Nonprofessionals are held to the "reasonable man" standard, while professional are held to a higher standard. For professionals, "The standard of care expected of a professional has traditionally been viewed as that of the ordinarily competent member of that profession" (Car and Williams, "Computers and Law" [Intellect: 1994] at page 240).

The roots of this discrepancy lie in the massive information advantage that professionals have over their clients. This information advantage gives the professional an opportunity to take advantage of the unknowing client.

The courts, however, have been reluctant to give programming a professional status. In *Pezzillo v. General Telephone & Electronics Information Systems, Inc.*

(572 F.2d 1189 1978), the court, using the definition of professional in the Fair Labor Standards Act of 1938, ruled that programmers were not professionals. In the decision, the court stated that programmers are analogous to drafters in that both perform mechanical functions (Scott, *Computer Law* [Wiley and Sons: 1989] at pages 7–14).

One of the necessary elements of a profession is a unified body of knowledge. Another is that the members of the profession organize to promulgate codes of behavior and the like. The education of programmers varies widely. Organizations like CPSR and the ACM do promulgate professional standards.

It is our conclusion that computer programmers should be considered professionals because they possess a technical skill that should be used with great care and thought. This determination would give them a higher duty of care to meet in their work.

## PRIVACY—HOW TO EXCLUDE AN AGENT

### Robots Exclusion

Sometimes people find that they have been indexed by an indexing robot or that a resource discovery robot has visited part of a site that for some reason shouldn't be visited by robots. In recognition of this problem, many Web robots offer facilities for Web site administrators and content providers to limit what the robot does. An early attempt to solve this were the following:

> *The Robots Exclusion Protocol:* A Web site administrator can indicate which parts of the site should not be visited by a robot, by providing a specially formatted file on the site, in http:// . . . /robots.txt.
>
> *The Robots META tag:* A Web author can indicate whether a page may or may not be indexed, or analyzed for links, through the use of a special HTML META tag.

Note that these methods rely on cooperation from the robot and are by no means guaranteed to work for every robot. If you need stronger protection from robots and other agents, you should use alternative methods such as password protection.

### The Robots Exclusion Protocol

The Robots Exclusion Protocol is a method that allows Web site administrators to indicate to visiting robots which parts of their site should not be visited by the robot. This proposed standard is not in common use and is being superseded by W3C standards. It was an early attempt to provide control.

In a nutshell, when a robot visits a Web site, say http://www.foobar.com/, it firsts checks for http://www.foobar.com/robots.txt. If it can find this document, it will analyze its contents for records like

```
User-agent:*
Dcomputer agentsllow:/
```

to see whether it is allowed to retrieve the document. The precise details on how these rules can be specified and what they mean can be found in the following:

Web Server Administrator's Guide to the Robots Exclusion Protocol

HTML Author's Guide to the Robots Exclusion Protocol

The original 1994 protocol description, as currently deployed

The revised Internet-Draft specification, which is not yet completed or implemented

## The Robots META Tag

The Robots META tag allows HTML authors to indicate to visiting robots whether a document may be indexed or used to harvest more links. No server administrator action is required. Note that currently only a few robots implement this, and it will shortly be superseded by new W3C standards.

In this simple example,

```
<META NAME="ROBOTS" CONTENT="NOINDEX, NOFOLLOW">
```

a robot should neither index this document nor analyze it for links. Full details on how this tag works are provided in

Web Server Administrator's Guide to the Robots META tag

HTML Author's Guide to the Robots META tag

The original notes from the May 1996 Indexing Workshop

# Agents in Use

*People react to new technology in three different stages:*
1. *"It's crazy and don't waste my time"*
2. *"It's possible, but not worth pursuing"*
3. *"I've always said it was a good idea"*

—Arthur C. Clarke

*Ours is the age which is proud of machines that think, and suspicious of men who try to.*

—H. Mumford Jones

*The rise of rule-based expert systems in the 1980s was predicated on the idea that computers could do what human experts could do, only less expensively. Those interested in trying out the then-new expert-system technology were told that the first problem tackled should be do-able by a person in more than an hour and less than a week.*

*Today, the emphasis is not on doing what people do. Instead, the emphasis is on exploiting opportunities to do tasks that people cannot do alone."*

—Excerpt from MIT briefing on the changing role of AI, 1997

The last quote puts into context the changes that are taking place in the use of Artificial Intelligence. Those changes have been brought about by the advent of a communications universe, the Internet, and the need now for intelligence to be applied to the many issues of inhabiting such a diverse medium.

Marshall McLuhan said, "The medium is the message." The message that is rapidly coming home to those early adopters of the Internet is that they need help to make it work for them. Tools are rapidly emerging in a range of areas to assist the Internet traveller in every aspect of his or her journey.

This section explores in more detail the areas of business that can most benefit from agent technology, the tools emerging, and the directions that development appears to be taking.

# 8

# How Will We Use Agents?

The key questions for the success of software agents are how and where will they be used and for what purpose. These are crucial questions for the acceptance and integration of any technology, and they require analysis and discussion.

Broadly, we see the areas—some will be rapid and others less so—for the introduction of agents.

1. **PC users.** By far the biggest area and the location where commercial products will concentrate on for market share (see statistics in Chapter 3). Personal computers continue to evolve with speed and capacity. Internet growth is related to sales of PC's. Estimates put the sales of PCs to be phenomenal, but when you consider that less than 1 percent of the entire world population has access to or uses computers at this time.
2. **Internet-based users.** Agents will help manage the use of the Internet, in Electronic Commerce, together with providing assistance with filtering, locating quality information.
3. **Corporate users.** Developing agents for their own commercial use. We see this in multiple areas such as Internet use, internal searching of private networks, assisting end users, and management of office tasks such as calendaring, scheduling, filtering e-mail, and multiple other uses.

## GENERAL APPLICATIONS OF AGENTS

It is pertinent at this stage to review broadly the application areas of agent technology. It is important to gain an understanding of the very large scope that this technology can have. We can define eight broad categories of agent use:

1. Personal Use
2. Network management
3. Information and Internet access

4. Mobility management
5. E-commerce
6. Computer User interface
7. Application development
8. Military applications

## Personal Use

As the power, capacity, and speed of the personal computer increase, there is a very strong need to introduce agents to help in the management of the personal computer. Agents can help with setting up scheduling appointments, file management, locating information, suggesting new ways to locate information and many others. We see agent technology making a big impact on the desktop and fully expect to see a variety of agents on every new computer that is shipped in the future.

## Network Management

As private, corporate, and Internet use continues to expand and become more complex, we see the need for agent technology to manage the technical network architecture and manage the traffic (rerouting when transactions volume becomes heavy). They can be used to manage data, files, web page content—as well as hardware, by locating printers, fax machines, and copiers.

## Information and Internet Access

As we discussed in Chapter 1, the information explosion and the need to establish sound management practices for accessing this information are very important for ensuring orderly success of Internet access. Agents are already providing services to manage, filter, select, prioritize, reroute, discard, monitor, and share information of all types. In addition, agents can suggest ways to get the best quality information by the quickest, most reliable route.

## Mobility Management

People in today's society are highly mobile and becoming more transient. Therefore, there is a need to manage the infrastructure so that remote users can access all the software, services, and facilities that make them productive and useful. Agents will help access software, suggest and improve applications, and look for resources on the network.

## E-Commerce

The promise of electronic commerce is causing most corporations to rethink how they do business and is being stimulated by the growth of Internet. The prospect of buying and selling goods and services electronically means that it will be done fast, thanks to automation. This simply means that there will be higher profits. The selection of products, building specifications, negotiating the best price, billing and collecting money from the customer immediately, and many other processes can all be achieved with agent technology. E-commerce is available not simply for large corporations with huge mainframe computers but also to anyone who can access the Internet.

## Computer User Interface

Agent technology will make the interface between the computer and the user much more usable and, most importantly, easier to access. Clearly, despite major advances in the past twenty years in interface design, there is still much progress to be made. Simply put, we have to make the communication with computers easy to use and understand, less confusing, more intuitive. This is another important area where agent technology will play a significant part. Agents will understand our preferences, learn and interpret, suggest changes or shortcuts, and make intelligent decisions. In the future, we can expect agents to adopt personalities that are agreeable and pleasing (also soothing), which interact with our best interests.

## Application Development

Agent technology shows great promise in assisting the development, design, and creation of commercial software—the process we call application development. Agents can find programs, code, modules, designs, specifications, and other technical tools to create future applications. Large, dynamic, complex, and distributed applications should be the first targets for software agent developers.

## Military Applications

The military establishment is very interested in anything that has intelligence. Agents, like their human counterparts, can be secretive in gathering sensitive information. The military and intelligence communities have been quietly deploying agent technology to gather information about our enemies and to transmit it for subsequent analysis. These software spies are expendable, require no food or water, are reliable, and work twenty-four hours a day, seven days a week. Agent technology gives a whole new meaning to the phrase "secret agent."

These are very broad categories designed to give an understanding of the breadth and range of where agent technology can and is being utilized. We shall examine more specific and individual applications in greater detail in this Section.

## COMPETITIVE INTELLIGENCE

Competitive intelligence is a relatively new technology, which is beginning to gain interest in the boardrooms of many corporations around the world. It is also high on the hype cycle of new technologies. Basically, competitive intelligence is about knowing more about your competitors, what they are doing, how they are doing it, and most important, how it might affect your business. Intelligence is different from information, which is different from data, as the following equation illustrates.

$$\frac{\text{DATA} = \text{INFORMATION} = \text{KNOWLEDGE} = \text{INTELLIGENCE}}{\text{INCREASING VALUE}}$$

Regrettably, the power of the competitive intelligence concept is often diluted because the definition itself is ill-defined or misunderstood and is used out of context. Popular business magazines frequently use the labels "data," "information," and "intelligence" interchangeably. This use is confusing to the average manager. This is also a sign that the technology is not well developed, that there are no standards, and are subject to rapid change.

Why is competitive intelligence important? The business pace of technological development and the growth of global trade mean that today's business environment changes more quickly than ever before. Corporate managers and executives can no longer afford to rely on instinct or intuition when making strategic business decisions. In almost all industries, the consequence of making one wrong decision may be that the company goes out of business. The need to have information that is reliable, accurate, and beneficial in decision making is critical for a business to be successful and profitable.

We define competitive intelligence as "a formalized, yet continuously evolving process by which the management team assesses the evolution of its industry and the capabilities and behavior of its current and potential competitors to assist in maintaining or developing a competitive advantage" (Prescott and Gibbons, 1993). Competitive intelligence tries to ensure that the organization has accurate, current information about its competitors and a plan for using that information.

There are three distinct phases in competitive intelligence:

1. Data harvesting
2. Analysis
3. Conclusion and action

Now that corporations have high-speed access to the Internet, they can accumulate a vast amount of data, harvesting from a vast array of sources. The following list is only a small sample of sources:

| | |
|---|---|
| Industry experts and analysts | Market and brokerage reports |
| Customers and clients | Television and radio |

Trade shows and conference papers    Private investigations
University research programs           Buyers' guides, catalogs
Annual reports, 10Ks                  Brochures/advertisements, Web
Newly enacted or pending              sites
legislation                           Internal experts/professional col-
Federal, state, local filings         leagues
International filings                  Supplier/vendor networking
Local, national, and international    Employees sales call reports
newspapers                            Online databases
Import/export statistics              Credit bureau reports
Court documents and filings           Industry directories
Freedom of Information Act            Recruitment want ads
Patent filings                        Special interest groups (SIGS)
Bankruptcy filings                    Political groups
Chapter 11 filings                    Biographies and profiles

As a competitive intelligence resource, the Internet serves both as a vital source of information and a cost-effective means of sharing and disseminating information to decision makers. Information-using agents can be harvested quickly. Almost all the sources described in the list are now available on the Internet, and agents can be used to collect specific information ready for analysis.

Analysis of this information can take many different forms such as benchmarking, comparative analysis, and scenario expansion. The analysis techniques chosen will depend on the output or deliverable required. Another example is sustainability analysis, which is a new method in competitive strategy that incorporates the different effects of time on the creation and erosion of business advantage. Sustainability analysis can provide early warnings of changing "rules of the game," especially in complex or shifting businesses. Such early warnings can mean competitive advantage.

The conclusion, the final stage of competitive intelligence, should clearly state what action is to be taken. It should define the outcomes in a report, presentation, or other format. It may take the form of a SWOT analysis—Strengths, Weaknesses, Opportunities, Threats. SWOT analysis is an effective method of identifying the positive or negative outcomes of the opportunities or threats that every corporation faces at some time.

### Case Studies

**1.** The NutraSweet Company, manufacturer of NutraSweet brand sweetener and other food ingredients, is a business unit of the giant Monsanto Company. The sweetener was discovered in 1965 by a researcher, James Schlatter, at G. D. Searle & Co. The CEO of the corporation, NutraSweet Company, estimates that he saves $50 million a year by using competitive intelligence techniques to assess business risk and to make acquisitions.

**2.** We would not expect competitive intelligence (CI) to be widely used in China. It is a new discipline in that country, where, despite a booming economy, many aspects of competitive business remain a novel concept. A large, state-owned enterprise applied CI to adapt to the presence of market competition, providing insight into how Chinese companies appraise the competitive strength of competitors and use this information to create competitive strategies. CI in China has an emerging role in university academics and business consultants.

**3.** Digital Equipment Corporation's computer systems division used competitive intelligence for business advantage in 1994–1995. In moving from a functional to a product-oriented business model, Digital employed competitive intelligence to analyze and evaluate new organizational designs and business process systems by defined market segments and competitors, and by projecting accepted economic principles. CI research efforts included information on competitive positions, potential shifts in product line positioning, tradeoff scenarios from one system type to another, pro forma investment, and market share analyses.

### Agent and Competitive Intelligence

The concept of competitive intelligence is a natural complement to agent technology.

For more information see:

Society of Competitive Intelligence Professionals - SCIP
http://www.scip.org

This homepage features SCIP publications, electronic discussion groups, expert/speaker database, events calendar, and information about the organization. It is an excellent starting place for more information.

## Tasks

The next question that arises, given the descriptions just outlined, is, For what types of tasks will agent technology be used? Again, we can broadly define a number of areas. However, applications that may rely on software agents are used to solve highly complex problems and, in most cases, to carry out tedious, day-to-day, boring but essential tasks.

Characteristics of tasks that software agents are suited to handle include the following:

- Complexity
- Distribution and delivery
- Time criticality
- Dynamic nature
- Uncertain or changing environments

- Multiple objectives
- Multiple ways of solving problems
- Information overload
- Handling high volume of data
- Global connectivity
- Routine, repetitive and boring tasks

A good example of the use of an agent is in customer service. A question sent to Time, Inc., generated the following e-mail response immediately:

Subject:
    fortune archive question [GEN1998062800000028]
Date:
    Sun, 28 Jun 1998 15:11:50 GMT
From:
    service@pathfinder.com
To:
    tonyj@wow.net

Dear tonyj@wow.net:

Thank you for contacting Pathfinder Customer Service.

Your message was received at 11:11:50 on 06/28/98 and was assigned the tracking number GEN1998062800000028. Please note your tracking number also appears in the subject field of this email.

Your message will be forwarded to a representative as soon as possible for review. If you would like to visit Pathfinder's online help area, please point your browser to:

http://www.pathfinder.com/help

We appreciate your interest in the Pathfinder Network and look forward to serving you soon.

Pathfinder Customer Service

http://www.pathfinder.com/help
help@pathfinder.com
804.261.1425

This was clearly the work of a simple agent that acts upon incoming e-mails, responds to them, and forwards the messages to an appropriate person for action.

In the future, that person is likely to be replaced by another agent with a specific knowledge area of expertise.

## MOBILITY

One of the main issues regarding the future of agent development is whether mobility is a benefit or a curse. There are many reasons to believe it is the latter. While it is true that agents working on other systems distribute the load, the problems that this idea presents are legion.

First let's consider the issue of permission. Say that an agent migrates to your server with the task of compiling a complete index of every word and sending it back to home base (or even worse, storing it locally like a giant cookie file). Are you sure you want that load on your system plus that space taken up? In the space of a day, 10,000 such agents may wish to run and bring your server down. So how do you accept a friendly agent that you might want (say from Yahoo, finding out what your site was all about to make it easier for people to get there)?

The second consideration is security. How do you limit what that agent can do once you have given it permission? Currently the agent operating from home base is limited to exploring your HTML pages for information, but an agent running on your server . . . hmmm.

Third, there is the issue of writing these agents when the servers on the web vary so greatly from NT to Unix to AS400 to Mainframe, all with their own language restrictions. It is OK to say Java, but there may not be a Java Virtual Machine running.

Finally, other than distributing load, there is the argument that there is little gain for such a large risk. Although it is true that there will be a need to run agents on remote systems, the argument can be made that these should be agents delivered by the remote host that your agent requests action from. This method would ensure that companies control their own agent universe and what the agents can do.

### Arguments for Using Mobile Agents

The following extract is from a key player in the area of mobility arguing for mobility. A company called General Magic.

The following arguments were taken directly from an e-mail by Danny Lange at General Magic. General Magic is one of the most knowledgeable companies working in the area of agent development. The arguments are good, but the security and control problems that have not yet been addressed will slow down for some time the move of agents into a truly mobile role.

> *They reduce the network load.*
>     Distributed systems often rely on communications protocols that involve multiple interactions to accomplish a given task. This is especially true

when security measures are enabled. The result is a lot of network traffic. Mobile agents allow you to package a conversation and dispatch it to a destination host where the interactions can take place locally. Mobile agents are also useful when it comes to reducing the flow of raw data in the network. When very large volumes of data are stored at remote hosts, these data should be processed in the locality of the data, rather than transferred over the network. The motto is simple: move the computations to the data rather than the data to the computations.

*They overcome network latency.*

Critical real-time systems such as robots in manufacturing processes need to respond to changes in their environments in real time. Controlling such systems through a factory network of a substantial size involves significant latencies. For critical real-time systems, such latencies are not acceptable. Mobile agents offer a solution, since they can be dispatched from a central controller to act loyally and directly execute the controller's directions.

*They encapsulate protocols.*

When data are exchanged in a distributed system, each host owns the code that implements the protocols needed to properly code outgoing data and interpret incoming data, respectively. However, as protocols evolve to accommodate new efficiency or security requirements, it is a cumbersome if not impossible task to upgrade protocol code properly. The result is often that protocols become a legacy problem. Mobile agents, on the other hand, are able to move to remote hosts in order to establish "channels" based on proprietary protocols.

*They execute asynchronously and autonomously.*

Often mobile devices have to rely on expensive or fragile network connections. That is, tasks that require a continuously open connection between a mobile device and a fixed network will most likely not be economically or technically feasible. Tasks can be embedded into mobile agents, which can then be dispatched into the network. After being dispatched, the mobile agents become independent of the creating process and can operate asynchronously and autonomously. The mobile device can reconnect at some later time to collect the agent.

*They adapt dynamically.*

Mobile agents have the ability to sense their execution environment and react autonomously to changes. Multiple mobile agents possess the unique ability to distribute themselves among the hosts in the network in such a way as to maintain the optimal configuration for solving a particular problem.

*They are naturally heterogeneous.*

Network computing is fundamentally heterogeneous, often from both hardware and software perspectives. As mobile agents are generally computer- and transport-layer-independent, and dependent only on their execution environment, they provide optimal conditions for seamless system integration.

*They are robust and fault-tolerant.*

The ability of mobile agents to react dynamically to unfavorable situations and events makes it easier to build robust and fault-tolerant distributed systems. If a host is being shut down, all agents executing on that machine will be warned and given time to dispatch and continue their operation on another host in the network.

# CHAPTER

## 9

# Health

*In the future, agents are going to be the only way to search the Internet, be-*
*cause no matter how much better the Internet may be organised, it can't keep*
*pace with the growth in information.*

—Bob Johnson, Dataquest, Inc.

For the purposes of simplicity, we can classify the process of medical diagnosis and treatment of disease into the following six categories:

1. **Diagnosis**—the understanding and identification of the problem.
2. **Treatment**—a set of procedures identified to correct the illness identified in diagnosis.
3. **Recuperation**—the process of recovering from the treatment and diagnosis.
4. **Follow-up**—a set of monitoring procedures that occur after treatment and recuperation to ensure that the solution is successful.
5. **Administration**—the management of the entire process from diagnosis to follow-up, and it refers to the process of making things happen and paying for them.
6. **Education**—learning about illness, preventing disease, new procedures, treatments, and so on.

In some cases, it might not be necessary to follow all these phases when dealing with an illness. The next question that arises is, **Where can agent technology be of assistance in the whole field of medicine?**

High-quality health care at low cost, improved outcomes, complete care coverage from the hospital to the home, and decision support for patients and health care teams are some of the crucial challenges for improving future health care worldwide. Services are being consolidated under larger enterprises of managed care where needs for primary care are rapidly displacing specialty care. Cost containment puts a strong emphasis on fewer patient visits, fewer diagnostic tests and procedures, and shorter hospital stays. The need has become acute for having up-to-date patient information readily available anywhere within the enterprise of care, including the home.

Imagine that a few years from now, you turn to your PC to call up the reminders and actions for the day from your personal desktop agent (PDA). The agent technology displays a number of reminders and occasions that you need to attend to, such as birthdays, social events, and appointments. Your medical agent for example, knows in detail all your medical history, the problems you are experiencing, and the treatments you need. It understands the medications that you need, automatically alerting and then refilling medications—checking first with the pharmacy agents that this is acceptable. It reminds you that you need to take your weekly medication today and that you have an appointment with your cardiologist at 3:00 P.M. today.

The following is a likely scenario. We'll call it "The Case of Jessica's Ear."

Jessica is a student who lives in Columbus, Ohio. She has developed painful ear problems resulting from frequent air travel and is in constant discomfort. Working for her final exams, she ignores it, until finally it becomes unbearable. She consults her Personal Medical Agent—PMA—and after describing her symptoms, it sets up an appointment for her to see a prominent ear, nose, and throat doctor. He is one of the best specialists in the country, and luckily his calendar agent notifies her that he is visiting Columbus for a conference the following week. Jessica's PMA contacts the doctor's office and transmits Jessica's entire medical history, notes, past treatments, drug allergies, and so on.

The doctor is able to review all of Jessica's history prior to the appointment. His diagnostic agent provides a preliminary diagnosis of possible causes, points to possible treatments, and plots a treatment strategy. When she visits the doctor's office, he makes a physical examination and reviews all the symptoms. He calls up his diagnosis agent and conducts a short dialog to authenticate the findings.

He agrees with the treatment and instructs his treatment agent to prescribe a series of antibiotics and steroids, but notes that Jessica is allergic to a certain steroid that must be avoided. The prescriptions are transmitted over the Internet to the pharmacy nearest Jessica's home and will be waiting for her to pick up.

The doctor's insurance agent (the software kind) prepares all the relevant billing information, which is automatically transmitted over the Internet to the insurance company.

Jessica's condition improves rapidly after just two days of taking the medication. She continues to take it for ten days, and her PMA has only to remind her to do so once. (The doctor's agent transmitted back to Jessica's agent all the records, treatment, and other data.)

Jessica passes her exams—with extra help from her exam agent.

Does this sound like science fiction? Maybe it does, but this scenario is entirely feasible and practical with the implementation of software agents. Current medicine is limited both by its understanding and by its tools, and we can improve them in many ways by using multiple types of agents that communicate with each other and across the Internet, performing automated tasks for the owners/users. Following is a description of just such a system being developed at Stanford University.

---

### An Intelligent Assistant for Patient Health Care

The Patient Advocate is designed to be an intelligent assistant for patient-centered health care. Residing on a home computer or special-purpose device and operating within an extended health-care information network, the Patient Advocate will extend medical expertise into the outpatient setting. It will have remote access to the patient's medical record, an understanding of the patient's health status and history, and a model of the patient's interest in health-related issues, preferences for modes and contents of interaction, etc.

The Patient Advocate is being designed to provide three kinds of functions. First, it will assist the patient in managing continuing ambulatory conditions, for example chronic problems such as diabetes, special normal conditions such as prenatal care, and wellness issues such as diet, exercise, and stress. Second, it will provide health-related information by allowing the patient to interact with the on-line health-care information network and scan media resources to suggest information of interest. Third, it will act as a remote triage point for clinical services by coordinating patient-relevant information such as reminding the patient when a visit to the clinic is indicated.

We describe a prototype of the Patient Advocate which is designed to support obstetrics patients at risk of gestational diabetes. It is important that the Patient Advocate is platform-independent, runs on widely available hosts, and has access to various Internet resources. Therefore, it is implemented in Java and is Internet accessible.

**Silvia Miksch, Kenneth Cheng, Barbara Hayes-Roth**

Knowledge Systems Laboratory (KSL), M/C 9020, Gates Computer Science Building 2A
Stanford, California 94305, email: miksch@hpp.stanford.edu

Conference Proceedings, copyright 1997 ACM

---

## CURRENT STATUS

Agents can and will play a valuable role in our future health care and health support. The statement in the box gives some idea of the direction in which agent technology is traveling in the field. Unfortunately, the medical use of technology lags very far behind the general world of technology. That is not to say that computers are not part of many innovative systems to support patients. Far from it, but integration is sadly lacking.

To understand this situation, we must consider the web of support services, each with its own needs, which surrounds the health care environment.

- Hospitals and large clinics use computers for medical records and billing, and often very specialized computer equipment for testing and diagnosis. Unfortunately, these are designed in isolation with no understanding of or interface to any kind of intelligent network structure. Thus, a total picture and an integrated vision of patient care are very hard to achieve.
- Hospitals are supported by payments from insurance companies and Medicare/Blue Cross/Blue Shield. These bodies have their own tracking and information needs that focus on issues such as fraud detection, pattern recognition, exception reporting, and effective payment collection management.
- Doctors and specialists often work in computer isolation, having too small a practice for other than a simple PC computer that is running a scheduling, patient records, and billing software package.
- Pharmacies also have their own requirements that cover such issues as inventory management, statutory reporting, labeling, and billing.
- Government agencies such as district nursing, aged support, child support, and social services are often without computers; of if they have them, they are focused on tracking the work habits and productive deployment of staff, as well as scheduling and regulatory issues of reporting.
- World bodies such as the World Health Authority are interested in the fluctuations in cases of a number of diseases and in the statistical evidence of health in nations.
- Laboratories that carry out screening and testing have systems which focus on reporting details, statistical analysis of trends, record keeping, and billing. The "advocate" project highlighted in this Chapter indicates the environment for their following study.
- Gymnasiums and other health centers regularly monitor attendees, using a variety of tools and techniques. Currently, none of this information filters through to health professionals. This could be a valuable source of accurate statistics such as, heart rate, blood pressure, and so on.

## FUTURE DIRECTIONS

The Stanford project outline in the accompanying figure shows some of the complex web of interaction that supports health care. As the Stanford project points out, all these elements play a part in health care, plus one other important player,

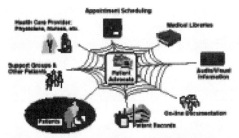

**Figure 1:** Several resources administered by the Patient Advocate project

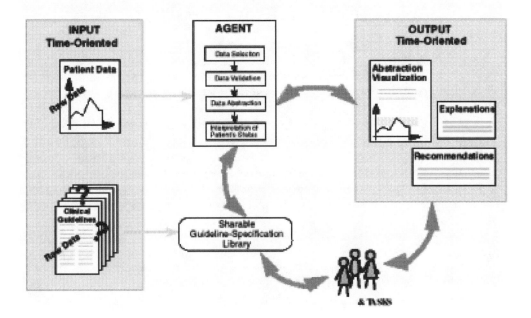

**The agent's system organization and its interactions**

the patient. The patient may well have a computer (one in three Americans does), but that computer is not oriented toward the patient's health care. Rather, it is used for a variety of home needs and is quite often used for work-related tasks. Of the computers that Americans have, approximately 25 percent are now connected to the Internet. The patient, therefore, more than the providers, is beginning to become positioned to have his or her health care supported by agent technology.

It is certainly likely that a home computer with an inexpensive add-on device such as a test unit that could monitor blood pressure, heart rate, and other factors could play a valuable part in preventive medicine for the majority and a vital service for those needing close monitoring. By utilizing the Internet, the patient could check health manuals, pass on vital signs via simple interactive entry screens as well as attached devices, and interact with the caring system to support all of the preceding interlinked services. The problem in this scenario is the present lack of a defined communications structure under which the various groups could begin to deliver the kind of service envisioned.

The scale of things makes this future scenario difficult. Health insurers deal with millions of claims and payments, and utilize large, old-fashioned mainframes to handle the raw processing power needed to take care of this volume. It will be very difficult and time-consuming for these systems to integrate into the Internet and directory with other providers.

Clinics run on minicomputers using Unix or on networked PCs. Hospitals, again because of the volume, have tended towards large machines that do not fit well into the modern Internet-driven idiom.

Pharmacies do not normally have sophisticated computer systems. The simple process of linking via a network to hospitals and downloading prescriptions is well beyond their scope. Doctors still have to write out prescriptions by hand.

We believe that the place where agent technologies will first emerge in the medical world is in hospital environments where the ability of an agent constantly to monitor and report has immediate impact. Currently, analogue devices are used to monitor patient care. These are expensive and difficult to maintain and are not integrated. Simple agent-based techniques that are supported by a PC network connected to the Internet (for monitoring by physicians and specialists away from the physical location) will emerge as cost-effective alternatives to existing tools.

Another area that is ready to emerge is that of patient-to-doctor online care. Just as in the banking world where online banking has been slow to start, needing the Internet (a common communications network) to kickstart, in medical care a natural link exists at the bottom of the health care chain between the patient and the doctor. This link can be exploited as both the patient and the doctor have equipment of similar scale. In a simple online scenario, the patient can interact with the doctor via semi-intelligent input screens that ask a series of questions to assist the doctor in analysis.

In work done at Miami University Medical Center in Ohio as far back as 1988, it was found that patients respond better to the anonymity of computer screen requests than they do to face-to-face interviews. This proven technique could therefore be used for prescreening and remote patient care and could extend the ability to serve beyond the current case load. Agents could play a valuable part in this with their ability constantly to monitor and to report; also, an agent can be patient-oriented and work with medical records, and the patient's own interactive input can begin to provide a valuable exception alerting functionality. This process would be greatly enhanced if such a simple monitoring device as just described were part of the system. These tools are now digital and used by many gymnasiums. They are inexpensive, and all that is needed is a PC link to capture data. Using this, a patient could provide regular monitoring information that the agent would assess and then report to the doctor any significant changes for action.

We would expect to see this kind of agent technology impact medical professionals initially in high risk-environments: patients who have known heart problems or degenerative diseases or who have a constant requirement for managing the status and impact of therapy.

Agents promise much progress in the automation of monitoring analysis and control of disease. This progress, along with the march of technological progress in new drugs and treatments, will herald new approaches to combating diseases.

# 10

# E-Mail

*The secret of success is knowing something nobody else knows.*

—Aristole Onassis

E-mail will be the first technology that will rival the telephone in popularity and use. Along with the explosive growth of the Internet, e-mail is set to grow to the same unprecedented levels of acceptance. As it becomes cheaper and more widespread, it will become a free service to most users. As this use explodes and as billions of messages buzz around the Internet, the use of agents will become important to manage and administer the volume and content of messages.

We predict the following:

- **Expanded e-mail services.** New services will be implemented such as multimedia messages that include video, sound, voice, and text. Delivery of new services will expand to other devices such as telephones, handheld terminals, pagers, and Webtv. The General Magic Initiative Portico described in Chapter 12 is the first major initiative in this area.
- **Based on the PC.** Despite the appearance of other new devices, the majority of e-mail will originate from the personal computer.
- **Use of agents.** New agent products and services will be needed to manage, control, and filter the enormous volume and content that this explosion will generate.

## GROWTH OF E-MAIL

In 1990, less than 2 percent of the population of the United States used e-mail. In 1996, that figure had leaped to 15 percent, or more than 40 million users. This exponential growth will continue to expand as more and more personal computers are linked to the Internet in order to communicate quickly and easily. See the accompanying figure.

A number of important factors are contributing to this growth in e-mail use:

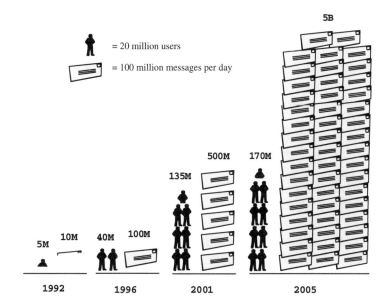

= 20 million users

= 100 million messages per day

**E-mail Access Grows and Message Volume Skyrockets (*Source: Forrester Research, Inc.*)**

- **Internet.** Access to the Internet implies the use of an e-mail service.
- **Use at work.** Many users are first exposed to e-mail at work. Workers enjoy the interaction of short, textual messages that eliminate the need for faxing or making photocopies.
- **Speed.** The ability to get fast responses across the globe is desirable.
- **Standards.** Almost all e-mail software can now talk to other software, and these open standards are contributing to the growth.

## THE ROLE OF AGENTS

Software agents will help with this digital deluge by administering, filtering, and generally controlling the volume of mail received. These processes include the following:

1. Controlling any unwanted, unsolicited e-mail or spam by rejecting or returning messages to their original owners. Any attempts to overload or fill up in-boxes will not be allowed.

2. Possibly prompting users by voice if certain designated messages arrive. An example might be, "The message you wanted from Brian in London has just arrived—shall I display it?" (This avoids those three dreaded words from cyberspace, "you've got mail.")

3. Fowarding mail messages to one or more destinations automatically—an example might be that all sales figures to the sales department.

4. Consolidating mail from numerous sources or locations.

5. Searching the Internet for new sources of news, stocks, or deals, and then delivering by e-mail.

6. Distinguishing from private/personal and corporate/business mail.

7. Automatically answering mail and responding according to conditions:
   "I'm currently in a meeting until. . . ."
   "I'm on vacation until. . . . Brian in London will get this message."
   "This subject will be dealt by. . . ."
   "My agent will automatically make an appointment for you."
   And many custom messages that meet conditions suitable to the users

8. The regular administrative tasks of desktop e-mail such as backing up files archiving, indexing for future searching.

## CONCLUSIONS

Electronic mail, as those corporate mail junkies have discovered, has two distinct advantages over the telephone:

- It can be read at your convenience.
- It is a permanent record.

The disadvantages are the:

- Absence of dialog
- Lack of "personality"
- Need to type
- Lack of urgency

E-mail will be able to alert the receiver, either soon through digital computer phones such as the newly announced. Nokia or later when Irridium (the satellite service) takes off, directly from your wrist.

The direction of computers is toward voice solutions. Above, we stated that 50 percent could be delayed. This trend will remove two disadvantages of mail, the need to type and the lack of personality. Combine this development with the growth of digital camera technology, and video e-mail becomes likely that will have a huge impact on x-rated services.

As far as we are aware, no one has done any published research on current telephone usage to discover what percentage could be e-mail and what requires voice contact. We suggest that probably over 50 percent could be time-delayed and therefore e-mailed. This trend is particularly likely if a cost of zero is applied to the latter, which is relatively the case with Internet use, since it is charged on a monthly basis rather than on usage.

The number of telephone calls globally is 250 million a day or 9,000 billion a year. As we have shown earlier, e-mail is currently in the 100-million-a-year area. The Internet itself is doubling about every six months so; if we use this as a yard-stick, we would see this usage in less than five years.

The impact of this explosion alone, not counting e-commerce on the telephone companies, is unknown at this point, but it indicates massive growth in long distance service structure and a decline in telephone switching service requirements.

# CHAPTER

# 11

# Finance

*The empires of the future are the empires of the mind.*

—Winston L. S. Churchill

## INTRODUCTION

In what way could computer agents help with our personal finance?

The growth of software packages to manage personal assets and money has been phenomenal. Quicken became the first finance package to break the million-user barrier and now has some 10 million users, and Microsoft Money is not far behind. These packages help individuals and families better manage their own finances. According to Microsoft, there are 4 million users of online banking using Microsoft's software alone.

These financial management packages are linking very rapidly to a diverse number of data sources to better support family and personal finance decisions.

### Stock Prices

Links to stock prices provide the ability to update personal portfolios of shares. This technology was originally designed as a help for asset management and total net worth statements. However, agent technology now makes it possible for these links to automate alerts when prices of individual shares rise or fall below set limits and to trigger a buy or sell recommendation.

Both Microsoft and Quicken have implemented limited "goal-setting" agents. In this context in the future, these agents might manage a portfolio with the instruction to "maximize long-term growth over immediate returns."

### Banks

Banks are rapidly realizing that customers do not want another piece of software for one specific bank to manage their accounts remotely. Such software is too specific. Many people bank with more than one bank; also, the learning curve of special software and the inability of that software to link to other home finance software are very limiting.

Quicken and Microsoft (which may end up buying a bank so that the software can be more closely linked) are working with banks to link their products into the banks' networks. According to Microsoft, over one hundred leading U.S. banks are interfacing with Microsoft Money.

### Finance Companies

Links to finance companies provide competitive loan and mortgage information, and provide the ability to ensure payments on time, as well as providing better choice of instruments.

### Insurance Companies

These links provide competitive insurance opportunities for a wide range of requirements. Many people do not regularly review home, car, and personal insurances because of the time that it would take and the effort that is involved. Agents working within the money manager software can facilitate these decisions and provide access to highly competitive options.

### Tax Planning

Agents can work with your finance package to minimize your tax exposure.

## TYPES OF AGENTS

Agents, then, provide a number of possibilities:

- Reminders of bank account limits and time-specific items such as rollovers and payments
- Opportunities, promotions, and specials
- Automated transfers and e-payments for a wide range of goods and services
- Best use of deposits, automatically reviewing on a daily basis the various banks' offerings and placing assets most effectively to maximize interest
- Mortgage updates and best prices
- Insurance updates and best prices
- Tax advice and alerts to tax-oriented, time-dependent information
- Pension planning and advice

Many of these services are available today from the leading software vendors.

In these tasks, the money manager agents will of course be interacting with bank agents tailored to sell their services.

### Investor Insight™ from Quicken

This is a powerful investment decision-making tool from Intuit, the makers of Quicken. Investor Insight helps you make better investment decisions by giving you tools to track, analyze, and manage your investments from your desktop computer. It's a service for investors who want to stay on top of their investments. With Investor Insight, you can:

Download news stories from the top news sources: Dow Jones News Service, PR NewsWire, and Business Wire.

Get five years of price histories for any company or mutual listed on the NYSE, AMEX, or NASDAQ, plus thousands of mutual funds.

Display charts and reports that show the price performance of each investment, comparisons with other investments, and percentage change over time periods.

Create personalized reports that provide an overview of all your investments and find out how they are doing.

Order in-depth company reports online.

Create custom indexes to track trends in a group of stocks or mutual funds.

### Online Banking from Quicken

The accompanying illustration shows how Quicken interfaces with a bank to coordinate your personal finances.

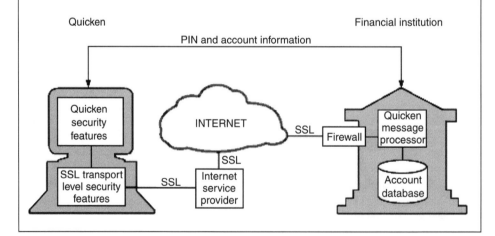

# 12

# Information

*With so much information now online, it is exceptionally easy to dive in and drown.*

—Alfred Glossbrenner

## INTRODUCTION

As our lives become more time driven and structured, our demands for information increase. Software agents offer a way to get the right information and to get it when required.

From the business viewpoint, agents will help the alert companies to identify customers' requirements in new ways. When you walk into a bookstore and browse, do not find what you want, and then leave, the bookstore management has no idea how to provide the service you need. When you or your agent browse via the Internet, the service provider has an opportunity to capture the request and, through analysis of the request, to improve service.

Our personal needs for information can be broken down into a number of areas.

### Health

Agents can be very useful in health care services. On the individual level, the Internet has provided us with a way to be connected into health care services. This process is not in existence yet, but costs alone (the cost of individuals' attending care and staff to attend them) will create the opportunity rapidly. In an expanding health care universe, with the trend of care being towards individual choice and responsibility, agents could

Find us the best price/performance care services.

Find us the best insurance coverage.

Work with providers to monitor our health.

Remind us of health care time-critical events (such as shots or checkups).

## Education

ZDNet University is one of the most interesting of a slew of new education opportunities on the Internet. For $4.95 a month, you can attend any of the classes currently running in a wide variety of technical subjects. Opportunities of this kind are springing up from traditional education sources, universities and colleges, correspondence companies, and new entrants with innovative approaches such as ZDNet.

Agents in this area could operate at many levels. Finding the right course at the right price is the obvious first choice as the number of offerings multiplies. Once you are enrolled, agents could be valuable servants to alert the busy student to classes and deadlines as well as sources of material required, for example, find me all the material on the development of HTTP standards.

## Automobiles

The world of auto purchasing is rapidly changing. Software agents can now take detailed specifications of your likes and dislikes and find you what you want.

Agents can search for the right vehicle at the right price, or the right part (particularly useful for enthusiasts), and also monitor vehicle Web sites and alert you when the vehicle you are interested in, at the price you wish to pay, becomes available. On the other side of this equation, the vehicle sites can interrogate the agents and find out the demand to actively fulfill your needs.

## Vacation/Travel

There are several opportunities for advanced agents in the travel area. Simple agents which track flights booked and update on status e.g. "your flight is delayed 4 hours", to more complex agents which monitor special offers for specific vacation packages or flight points and respond to criteria set by the user e.g. let me know when flights from Boston to New York are available on Fridays for less than US$50, or I wish to go to New York for a week which hotels are offering special packages during the following dates and what are they?

## Homes

There are two areas where agents can help in the property world. Property companies are rapidly proliferating on the Internet, and the ability to display your house to the world or to search for a house is constantly expanding. In this area, agents can be constantly vigilant on your behalf and can let you know when the ideal home is available. The other area is that of house support and maintenance. Agents can search on your behalf and find a wide range of goods and services, from companies offering solar heating, or to purchasing an antique washstand.

## Partners

This is an area where agent technology is set to mushroom. Globally there are already thousands of Web sites offering partner classified advertising and partner services. Currently there are companies making a lot of money out of the ability to deliver specific matches to someone seeking a partner. This is an ideal environment for an agent that would poll the sites on a regular basis and return a detail list of possible matches for follow-up.

## Sexual Gratification

X-rated services have been one of the greatest growth industries on the Internet and one of the few Internet businesses that have been profitable. Agents are used in increasingly sophisticated ways for men and women to find the sexual content of their choice. These are currently search and consolidate agents that scout the x-rated sites for specific content based on categories or word searches and that return to the user the matching pictures. Many x-rated sites have few real pictures and a lot of advertising, which is slow to load. Also, not all sites use thumbnails, often just giving the visitor a list of numbers to click on. A site with one hundred or more photos can be very tiresome; until you have loaded each image, it is impossible to tell whether it is of interest. There are now agents available that will visit a selected number of sites and retrieve the pictures for you, thumbnail them, and present you with an album with which to browse.

## Employment

The application of agent technology to aid the process in funding employment has particular benefits. Many websites now exist for funding the right job. The accompany diagram is one example of many available.

One of the most aggressive users of intelligent agents has been the job search community. Agents such as "swoop" from the monster board (monster.com) allow a job seeker to identify the kind of work that the person is looking for, as well as the person's skills, and the agent will monitor the job market and alert the person via e-mail of any jobs that match the criteria. An example is shown here, from the search words "Manager" and Director"

```
30-JAN-98 Operations Manager  Salem Hospital
30-JAN-98 Manager Strategic Planning V International
30-JAN-98 Project Coordinators In Focus Systems
30-JAN-98 Project Leader- Information Systems SCHERING-PLOUGH LABORATORIES
30-JAN-98 Project Leader- Information Systems SCHERING-PLOUGH LABORATORIES
30-JAN-98 Project Managers    Keane, Inc.
30-JAN-98 Solution Center Manager    KPMG Peat Marwick LLP
30-JAN-98 Information System Specialist    RW Steen Associates
30-JAN-98 TECHNICAL MANAGER   Network Communications, Inc.
30-JAN-98 Senior Oracle Applications Manager Seagate Software
```

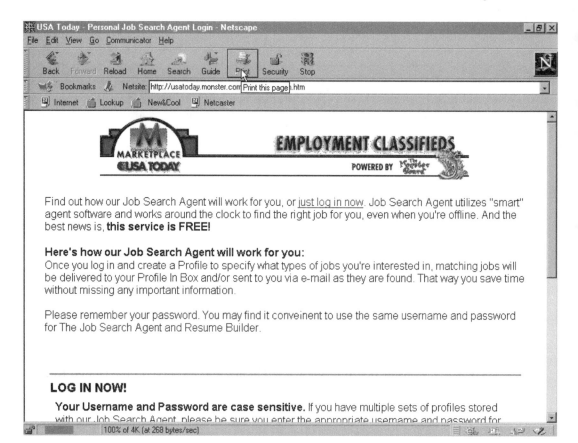

```
30-JAN-98 Application Team Manager     Kmart
30-JAN-98 Application Team Manager     Kmart
30-JAN-98 Application Team Manager     Kmart
30-JAN-98 Project Manager       CENDANT
30-JAN-98 Application Team Manager     Kmart
30-JAN-98 Application Team Manager     Kmart
30-JAN-98 Project Leader- Information Systems SCHERING-PLOUGH LABORATORIES
30-JAN-98 Network Manager       American Civil Liberties Union
30-JAN-98 Student Systems Consultants Business Information Technology Inc
30-JAN-98 PeopleSoft Consultants       Business Information Technology Inc
30-JAN-98 Application Team Manager     Kmart
30-JAN-98 Application Team Manager     Kmart
30-JAN-98 Application Team Manager     Kmart
30-JAN-98 Application Team Manager     Kmart
30-JAN-98 Application Team Manager     Kmart
30-JAN-98 Application Team Manager     Kmart
30-JAN-98 Conseillers dex pirience     AGTI Consulting Services Inc
```

```
30-JAN-98 Apprentice Mechanic City of Oshawa
30-JAN-98 Network Management Technical Architect-B BellSouth Cellular Corp
30-JAN-98 WEB SITE ARCHITECT  ThoughtWorks
```

There were additional jobs that matched your profile. In order to provide
the best service to the 700,000 users that have profiles at The Monster
Board, we have had to limit the number of matches we send via e-mail to
100. We apologize for any inconvenience that this may cause. However,
please note that all jobs that match your profile are stored in your Profile In Box on The Monster Board.

These jobs are waiting in your Profile In Box right now.
For complete list of jobs, as well as descriptions of these jobs, and to
apply online, visit The Monster Board at: http://www.monster.com
Select the Job Search Agent and log in with your username and password.

Swoop will continue to scan the jobs database for new positions that match
your career interests and place them in your Profile In Box on The Monster
Board. You will continue to be notified in subsequent e-mails. If you no
longer want this e-mail notification, simply edit your Profile and click
"Do Not Notify By E-mail."

These agents have become a necessary part of job hunting because sites such as the Monster Board in the United States and Jobserve in the United Kingdom have thousands of jobs. Jobserve, which has only IT vacancies, has a regular base of 15,000 jobs and a daily turnover of 2,000 to 3,000. Searching each day by hand would be a laborious process. These sites allow the user quite sophisticated search techniques. Jobserve, for example, allows phrases in quotes, + for "must have" and – for "don't want," as well as a wide variety of other search contexts.

Unfortunately, the search engine technology of the Internet is still in flux, and all these sites appear to be using different search engines. For that reason, the job hunter has to learn many different systems' syntax, which is often confusing (for example, Jobsite, another large U.K. site, does not recognize words in quotes).

However, these agents are growing in sophistication. The Monster Board agent now offers clients the opportunity to search their own archive, plus any jobs on the news-group circuit. We would expect to see second generation derivatives develop here, as well as sites that do not have their own databases but allow a customer to search all other sites.

## Other Areas

### Missing Children

Every year, there are over 1 million cases of missing children, including approximately 500,000 child abduction cases in the United States. An abduction can happen to a child at any time or any place, when parents least expect it. Millions of families suffer the pain, anguish, and trauma of this catastrophe. Each day 2,300 missing children are reported to local police and entered into the Federal Bureau of Investigation's National Crime Information Center computer system. The National Center for Missing and Exploited Children (NCMEC) based in Arlington, Virginia, is dedicated to help recover these missing children and to prevent other children from becoming victims of abduction and sexual exploitation. It is the United States' main resource center for child protection. It spearheads national and international efforts to locate and recover missing children and raises public awareness about ways to prevent child abduction, molestation, and sexual exploitation. A private, nonprofit organization established in 1984, NCMEC operates under a congressional mandate and works in conjunction with the U.S. Department of Justice's Office of Juvenile Justice and Delinquency Prevention.

NCMEC has disseminated the photographs of millions of missing children, with one in seven of the children recovered as a direct result. NCMEC believes that "somebody knows where each missing child is located" and seeks to reach every home with these photographs.

When a child is reported missing, it is absolutely imperative that searches be immediate and comprehensive. Local law enforcement agencies devote much of their resources to find the missing child, and their efforts are truly remarkable. Unfortunately, law enforcement does not always have the resources to devote to

# DONNA MICHELE BARNHILL
## Nonfamily abduction

Age-progression
by NCMEC (4/94)

**Missing:** 03/18/81   **Race:** White
**Birthdate:** 04/19/67   **Hair:** Brown
**Sex:** Female         **Eyes:** Brown
**Missing from:** Lexington, NC

NATIONAL
CENTER FOR
**MISSING &**
**EXPLOITED**
CHILDREN

ANYONE HAVING INFORMATION SHOULD CONTACT
The National Center for Missing & Exploited Children
1-800-813-5678

these complex investigations that often last many years. The circumstances of abduction are frequently complex and cover many other agencies, such as the Federal Bureau of Investigation, U.S. Secret Service, U.S. Bureau of Alcohol, Tobacco, and Firearms, U.S. Customs Service, U.S. Postal Inspection Service, U.S. Marshals, and U.S. Drug Enforcement Agency.

The Internet has proven to be a valuable resource for locating children, with Web pages and the ability to give help, tips, and assistance quickly and easily. State and local agencies can post photographs with details asking Internet users for information and assistance. The NCMEC has developed sophisticated age projection software to depict how children might have changed over the years. The software takes photographs and manipulates the images to show how the child might have aged since the abduction or runaway. Now there is the hope of employing intelligent agent software to supplement the existing resources.

### How the System Works

This experimental system is the first application of intelligent agents that assist case managers to search the Internet for any information or data concerning missing children. Further, it will look for matches of photographs and images that match a profile of the missing child. The agents will automate many of the tedious and time-consuming tasks that case managers are faced with in locating children. There are two basic tools:

1. A facial recognition software tool that automates the matching of photographs with input from multiple Internet sources. Photographs are the key resource in locating children.
2. The intelligent agent facilitates the process of investigation, assessing the success of leads and anticipating the likelihood of success. It is a mobile agent that scans and searches the Internet using keywords and that then reports its results.

With so many people using the Internet, there is a great increase in the chances of success. With agent software, the odds are even greater.

# 13

# Banks

*Obstacles are those frightening things you see when you take your eye off your goals.*

—Henry Ford

Banks, both large and small, are flocking to the Internet. They now realize that the Internet is the preferred medium for potential new business. The huge growth in consumer purchases of PCs over the past decade has fed the expansion of online banking. By 1995, more than 30 million households in the United States had home computers. More than a third used some type of personal finance software such as Intuit or Quicken. The natural progression was to provide online access.

The market parameters are now the "triple A" banking (anytime, anywhere, anyhow) and the one-stop-financial-shopping experience. Online banking will allow banks to cut costs, get more business, and keep customers satisfied as well as automating many of the business transactions. Financial institutions are in a life-or-death race with technology, telecommunications, and other companies to provide home banking services. Electric, telephone, and cable companies already have lines into homes that can transmit financial information, and they are trying to develop new services. If customers can transfer money and get loans via a technology or communications company that already has lines into their homes, why would they need a bank? The race is on. Banks have also built, at tremendous expense, a lavish branch system that although shrinking, is still expensive to maintain. The investment in bricks and mortar has been substantial, and banks have to make good on these investments before they charge into new technologies. They must stay innovative enough to keep up with their increasingly computer-adventurous customers. It is a very thin line that most banks are walking. Understandably, banks have made many attempts at home banking before and have been experimenting since the early 1980s, most without success. But that was before the Internet. Now the race is engaged to provide the services and to make more profits.

Some early experiences are as follows:

- Wells Fargo, based in California, revealed that its online banking base grew from 20,000 to 270,000 users in the first eighteen months. They expect to have 2 million users within five years.
- South Umpqua Bank, a small bank in rural Oregon with just $200 million in assets, opened a "computer café" where customers access accounts, traverse the Internet, or simply sip the bank's own brand of coffee.
- BayBank of Boston, Massachusetts, attracted 100,000 subscribers to its PC banking program in its first three months of operation.
- APL, a small 8,000-member credit union in Laurel, Maryland, became the fifteenth institution in the world to offer Internet-based checking, and within four weeks had 10 percent of its members using it.
- American Express, with its 38 million cardholders, added merchant services and traveler's checks to its Express Net service.
- Old Kent Banking in Grand Rapids, Michigan, rolled out its Actionbank, an online banking system that includes voice recognition, telephone banking, Internet banking, direct-dial PC banking, bill-paying services, screenphone access, statement printing, ATM access, and postage stamps.

## AGENTS IN BANKING

We see a great future for agent technology in banking. The processes of banking lend themselves to the implementation of agents. Agent technology can assist and facilitate the processing of many banking transactions for simple inquiries. A banking agent could flash to a person's home computer a message that her car lease is about to expire and that asks if she wishes to refinance, or a message that her checking account has a balance of less than $100 and might go overdrawn.

Following is a sample of what can be achieved:

- **Locating the**
  Best value mortgage at the best rate
  Best commercial loans at the best interest rate
  Best loan for a car, truck, or other vehicle
  Right insurance and brokerage rates
- **Advice regarding**
  Confirmation on deposits, checks, funds of all types
  Buying the best stocks/bonds/CDs
  Matching the client with the best mutual funds
  Real estate recommendations—houses/condos/apartments
  Assistance in creating financial plans, investment portfolios
  Retirement planning, 401K and IRA selection

- **Administration, to**
    Generate and deliver statements on demand (to fax, PC, WebTV)
    Look for old checks or transactions in the archives
    Provide links to other services, financial sites of interest

The accompanying figure illustrates an array of banking services that can be provided by agents.

## Now the Bad News

Banks have been traditionally conservative about investing heavily in new technology and this is reflected with agent software. *There is not widespread acceptance or use of agents in the banking industry worldwide.* It will not stay for very long and it will take a few key banks to announce and introduce an agent service—and many others will follow. It will open the floodgates as everyone scrambles to introduce agent technology.

We recommend that you watch these specific banks for agent technology:

Chase Manhattan          American Express
Wells Fargo              Bankers Trust
Citibank                 PNC Bank
Bank of America          Barnett Bank

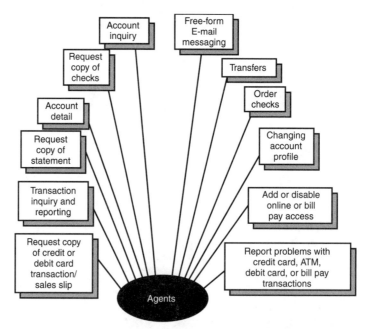

**A Simple Array of Agent Banking Services**

Visa International          J. P. Morgan
Mastercard

These are large national banks that have extensive resources, money, and Web presence to consumer agent technology.

## Integrion

Integrion Financial Network is a company created through an equal partnership of eighteen North American financial institutions, VISA U.S.A., and IBM Corporation. Integrion's founders share the following vision:

> The financial services industry needs an efficient channel for the processing and delivery of bank-branded electronic financial services. It is imperative that ownership and control of this channel remain within the financial services industry.
>
> The lack of industry standards is impeding development of the market for electronic financial services and is enabling software companies and third party processors to gain control over the payment system as well as position non-bank brands between financial institutions and their customer bases.
>
> A large-scale collaboration will create the critical mass to speed development of open standards, provide economies of scale and counter the encroachment of non-financial institutions into the payment system.
>
> Integrion, through the Interactive Financial Services Platform, offers financial institutions a network through which electronic transactions flow from multiple consumer access points to the banks host systems and/or processors. The Integrion owners, who collectively provide services to over 75 million U.S. households, are committed to creating an open platform with standards available to any and all providers. Equally important, the owners have made a commitment to provide access to Integrion to all financial institutions on an equal basis. Financial institutions who are not owners of Integrion will receive the same services, pricing levels and support as will owner financial institutions.

The participating Banks are as follows:

ABN AMRO North America, Bank of America, Bank One, Barnett Bank, Citibank, Comerica, First Chicago NBD, First Union National Bank, Fleet Financial, IBM, Key Corp., Mellon Bank, Michigan National Bank, NationsBank, Norwest, PNC Bank, Royal Bank of Canada, US Bancorp, VISA USA, and Washington Mutual Inc.

## CASE STUDY—A VIRTUAL BANK

**Problem:** With the intent of creating a successful future, BV a large German Bank Holding Company, decided to develop a completely autonomous "virtual bank" subsidiary (in that it has no brick and mortar branches) called Advance Bank AG.

BV needed to act quickly and did not have the depth of internal resources to do the project alone; therefore, it teamed with Andersen Consulting. The Advance Bank subsidiary was designed to attract new, higher income customers between the ages of 25 and 50 by offering a range of direct-banking services never before offered by the parent bank such as 24 hours a day, seven days a week (24×7) banking. Launched in March 1996, the new Advance Bank delivers a combination of flexibility, capability and convenience to its target market via telephone, fax and, as of May 1997, the Internet. Customers can do any kind of banking transactions, including paying bills, purchasing stocks, receiving financial information and managing household budgets.

**Objective:** With the goal of being more competitive, why would BV choose to open a virtual bank? If the parent bank had chosen to open another brick and mortar branch, it would have faced a new capital investment of up to Deutsche marks (DM) 3 million (about U.S.$2 million) that would have required up to 10–20 employees. With a branch bank operating only five days a week, 10 hours a day, branch comes with enormous fixed costs that are primarily unused. Therefore, Advance Bank's virtual branchless operation is a great direct cost savings. In comparison, BV, the parent bank, today has 770 branches mainly located in North and South Germany. Commerzbank, the closest competitor has more than 1,000 branches. To gain the same branch coverage as Commerzbank, BV would have needed to open 270 new branches—each at an investment of DM1 million to DM3 million (e.g., total investment of DM400 million to DM800 million).

Advance bank is an example of the rapid creation of a virtual enterprise to capitalize on a market opportunity to generate and fulfill demand. For example, the bank has established virtual business partners, extended the reach of its business to build new customer-focused relationships, and added revenue without the cost-investment of a branch network. Being virtual has also allowed Advance Bank to partner with other enterprises for noncore functions. For example, the data center, fulfillment center, and security processing and payments are supported by (outsourced to) companies other than Advance Bank. This enables Advance Bank to better focus on core competencies.

**Approach:** Andersen Consulting helped BV create Advance Bank in nine months—an amazingly short implementation time. Andersen Consulting's 100-person team, comprised of employees from many countries, was key in creating the infrastructure to support the bank's strategy. This included a component of major importance to delivering convenience and flexibility—the bank's call center, which lies behind its virtual facade. The call center transfers customer calls and data to highly trained phone human agents. These agents use communications and IT to answer complex inquiries, execute a broad range of financial transactions and provide independent financial consultation. The call center's success depends on the efficient use of communications and client/server technology. The solution was the effective integration of emerging technology, such as the Computer Telephone Integration (CTI), which allows the coordinated transfer of customer calls and call-related data between phone agents (see Note 1 for scope of the Advance Bank project).

### Note 1.   Scope of the Advance Bank/Andersen Consulting Project

1. Hardware and system software recommendation and purchase planning.
2. Data center office and call center infrastructure planning.
3. Implementation of a fault-tolerant client/server architecture to support banking operations in a 24×7 environment. Andersen's Foundation for Co-operative Processing (FCP) provided the applications development and deployment environment.
4. Integration of workflow and imaging functionality.
5. Call center implementation and integration, using corders.
6. Call center applications development for customer acquisition, customer care, investment services and general payment/banking transactions.
7. Selection of a new core banking system; modification to adapt the new, creative cash-management account; and integration with the front-end system. Extensive use of custom designed software agents.
8. Selection of services providers for data center, fulfillment (lettershop), securities and payment processing, and overflow call centers. Integration of the services providers to build the virtual corporation.
9. Training curriculum development and implementation of training materials for the call center personnel.
10. A new Internet customer channel, complete with full Internet banking services, recently went live to augment the initial phone and fax channels. In a year, Advance Bank plans to offer multimedia home banking to customers through integration of the Internet and the telephone.

**Results:** Since Advance Bank began with no customers, the 3,200 calls it received on "day one" of operation were all from prospects. By December 1996, less than one year after its launch, Advance Bank had more than 25,000 new customers (only 6 percent from its parent bank), 260 employees and more than DM1.3 billion in deposits (total assets are $765 million). The average portfolio is above DM100,000 ($63,000) and the average cash-management account has more than DM70,000 ($52,000). By the end of the year 2000, Advance Bank expects to have more than 800 employees and more than 250,000 customers.

Customers have around-the-clock access to by phone, fax, PC, and the Internet 24 hours a day, 7 days a week. Human interaction is always provided. In addition, 85 percent of the calls are answered in 15 seconds. This high level of personalized service is key to helping Advance Bank capture expanded market share. *In fact, the bank gained more assets in the first year than any other direct bank in Germany.*

Due to the low cost structure and flexibility of virtual banking, Advance Bank is able to offer a fresh product and service mix that focuses on customer relationships. One example is an innovative agent cash management account that earns interest on a customer's total deposits and allows him or her to allocate these funds in several different types of subaccounts for better budget management. This enables the customer to track personal expenses without the need for additional software.

**Conclusions:** The Advance Bank project is a good example that having the foresight and courage to "start from scratch" can be advantageous. Ingenuity and teaming with a systems integration partner for necessary skills to get the job done right in a timely fashion produced a successful new business for BV, delivering solid business results in a competitive market.

> Internet Address for Advance Bank AG
> http://www.advance-bank.de
>
> *Source:* Gartner Group Research Note: Nov 14, 1997.

## SUMMARY

It is very early days for the acceptance of agent technology in online banking. The American Bankers Association estimates that less than 3 percent of transactions were completed online in 1997. Many consumers are still wary of the privacy issues despite having the hardware and software to get online. Another big stumbling block is that merchants such as top retail department stores do not accept electronic payments. These problems will slowly erode as more and more consumers embrace the online world and find that it works. Agents will facilitate that process. Banks continue to be drawn to the Internet but have yet to embrace agents in a big way.

# CHAPTER

## 14

# Retail

Shopping online is about to explode as customers with personal computers and Internet access start to shop around and then purchase all types of goods and services. In a few years, Internet retail has come from almost nothing to substantial levels and volumes. This trend will continue, and one main but simple factor is driving this market—convenience. Users with personal computers who simply do not have the time to visit stores are finding online the variety and types of things they want. This trend is compelling and will continue to grow to record levels in the next five years.

To review, among the main reasons for on-line shopping are

- Convenience, speed, and access
- Choice of prices
- Greater selection
- Fast delivery options
- Growing confidence in value

Forrestor Research, Inc., conducted a survey of over 300 online shoppers and then analyzed the trends, habits, and other data. The results are shown in the accompanying figure. For example, security, once a major concern, does not detract from the main benefits of online shopping. Also as seen in the Figure, the current demographics are interesting. Expect to see these demographics change materially as other types of people and cultures get on the Net and start shopping.

Agent technology will supplement and expand this trend to provide greater choice and speed, together with the ability to filter and recommend.

## REVENUES

After a slow start, revenues are climbing dramatically. Dell Computer, for example, is processing over $4 million of computer sales in a week. That figure is expected to grow to over $7 million and trend upward even more in the next few months. (See the accompanying figure.)

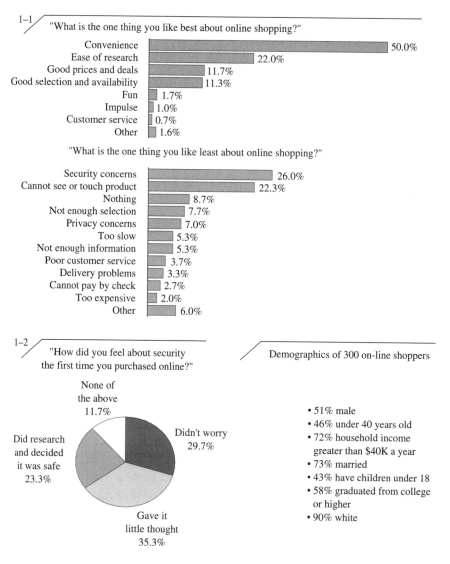

1–1
"What is the one thing you like best about online shopping?"

| | |
|---|---|
| Convenience | 50.0% |
| Ease of research | 22.0% |
| Good prices and deals | 11.7% |
| Good selection and availability | 11.3% |
| Fun | 1.7% |
| Impulse | 1.0% |
| Customer service | 0.7% |
| Other | 1.6% |

"What is the one thing you like least about online shopping?"

| | |
|---|---|
| Security concerns | 26.0% |
| Cannot see or touch product | 22.3% |
| Nothing | 8.7% |
| Not enough selection | 7.7% |
| Privacy concerns | 7.0% |
| Too slow | 5.3% |
| Not enough information | 5.3% |
| Poor customer service | 3.7% |
| Delivery problems | 3.3% |
| Cannot pay by check | 2.7% |
| Too expensive | 2.0% |
| Other | 6.0% |

1–2
"How did you feel about security the first time you purchased online?"

None of the above
11.7%

Didn't worry
29.7%

Did research and decided it was safe
23.3%

Gave it little thought
35.3%

Demographics of 300 on-line shoppers

- 51% male
- 46% under 40 years old
- 72% household income greater than $40K a year
- 73% married
- 43% have children under 18
- 58% graduated from college or higher
- 90% white

**Attitudes and Characteristics of Today's Online Shoppers. (*Source:* Forrester Research, Inc.)**

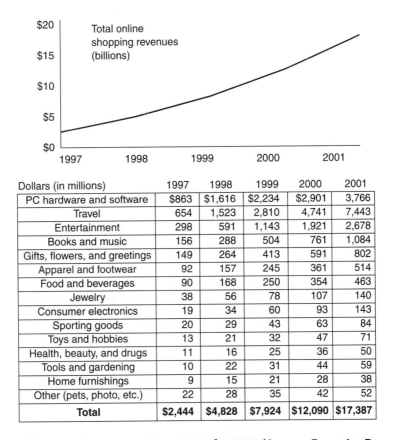

| Dollars (in millions) | 1997 | 1998 | 1999 | 2000 | 2001 |
|---|---|---|---|---|---|
| PC hardware and software | $863 | $1,616 | $2,234 | $2,901 | 3,766 |
| Travel | 654 | 1,523 | 2,810 | 4,741 | 7,443 |
| Entertainment | 298 | 591 | 1,143 | 1,921 | 2,678 |
| Books and music | 156 | 288 | 504 | 761 | 1,084 |
| Gifts, flowers, and greetings | 149 | 264 | 413 | 591 | 802 |
| Apparel and footwear | 92 | 157 | 245 | 361 | 514 |
| Food and beverages | 90 | 168 | 250 | 354 | 463 |
| Jewelry | 38 | 56 | 78 | 107 | 140 |
| Consumer electronics | 19 | 34 | 60 | 93 | 143 |
| Sporting goods | 20 | 29 | 43 | 63 | 84 |
| Toys and hobbies | 13 | 21 | 32 | 47 | 71 |
| Health, beauty, and drugs | 11 | 16 | 25 | 36 | 50 |
| Tools and gardening | 10 | 22 | 31 | 44 | 59 |
| Home furnishings | 9 | 15 | 21 | 28 | 38 |
| Other (pets, photo, etc.) | 22 | 28 | 35 | 42 | 52 |
| **Total** | **$2,444** | **$4,828** | **$7,924** | **$12,090** | **$17,387** |

**Online Retail Revenues Grow 700% by 2001 (*Source:* Forrester Research, Inc.)**

We predict that the estimates shown in the figure are *Conservative* and that the figures will be much higher as a result of the enablement of agent technology.

Not everything will sell on the Internet, and vendors are narrowing their focus to what sells well. Home furnishings, for example, are not a best seller, since people still prefer to go to the store to look and choose. However, books, music, and personal computers can be bought over the Internet with greater ease and comfort.

The following list represents some examples of the more successful players in Web-based online shopping:

Amazon Books                    1 800 Flowers
Virtual Vineyards               CDnow

Dell Computers                              Disney Store
The Sharper Image                           Cyperian
GardenEscape                                Outpost
Virgin Records                              Tower Records
JC Penney                                   LL Bean
CompUSA                                     Eddie Bauer
Gateway 2000                                Spiegel

## THE ROLE OF AGENTS

Today, the agent products for shopping on the Internet are still at a very early stage. These are still first-generation products.

Some samples include the following:

- **Jango.** Originally developed as a free personal computer product from Newbot that provides choice or products from categories such as books, cigars, wine, and coffee. Bought by Excite to be integrated into Excite shopping channels.

  http://www.jango.com/

- **Roboshopper.** This is an intelligent agent that makes online shopping fast and easy. The program automatically searches multiple online stores for a specific product and then displays the results in a convenient report so that the user can easily compare pricing and availability. RoboShopper can also search for product reviews and other information to help the user decide which product to buy. RoboShopper is distributed free of charge and is supported by advertising that is displayed while the product is in use. Also, it has a good general Web search summary feature that provides a summary of findings from the main search engines such as Excite, Alta Vista, and Yahoo.

  http://www.roboshopper.com/html/roboshopper.html

- **BargainFinder.** From Andersen Consulting's CSTR (Center for Strategic Technology Research) organization that conducts applied research to bridge the gap between emerging technologies and the business needs of their clients, this is an experimental Web page that users can access to find shopping bargains for CD music albums. Access to the top 40 selling albums as well as a list of music stores that BargainFinder selects is provided. As Andersen states, BargainFinder is as much an experiment in attitudes as in technology. We expect Andersen to expand into more specific commercial and retail products as a result of this research.

http://bf.cstar.ac.com/bf/

- **BottomDollar.** The Web page Bottom Dollar claims to find the lowest prices on the Internet in categories such as books, music, movies, hardware, software, and toys. Prices are current, since they are direct from the sellers.

http://www.bottomdollar.com/

- **BidFind.** This is a Web service that locates items in auctions. The user enters a keyword, and this is matched against current lists of items to be auctioned.

http://www.vsn.net/af/

- **Check It Out.** Check It Out™ refers to itself as the Web's best bargain finder. You may search the Web for products or merchants by keywords or phrases, browse categories, and see new listings, weekly specials, popular products, and new features.

http://www.checkitout.ca/

- **FIDO.** Fido provides a frequently updated, centralized database of vendor products and prices with a simple searching mechanism. Fido's database claims that it has over 100,000 consumer products from hundreds of vendors.

http://www.shopfido.com/

- **MX BookFinder.** This personal book-shopping service is an online bookstore comparison shopping agent designed to allow consumers to make informed decisions about purchases. Users can search for new, used, and out-of-print books. Also, a new minimum/maximum/feature allows users to give price ranges. Many bookstores online will be searched, and the results will be returned quickly. (This searches for books only.)

http://www.mx.org/bookfinder/

- **Advanced Book Exchange.** The Advanced Book Exchange claims that it is the Internet's most popular service for buying and selling out-of-print, used, rare, and antiquarian books. Users can create a profile of book interests, buy or sell books, and locate the best prices.

http://www.abebooks.com/

*Note:* These are typical examples of first generation agents that represent the first products providing services. We expect to see them grow in features and functionality.

## CRITICAL SUCCESS FACTORS

Following is a list of key issues that must be taken into account when designing and implementing shopping agents.

- **Buying/Selling.** Agents must be able to handle money transactions in a secure way with multiple currencies.
- **Negotiation protocols.** These are examples of protocols that facilitate commerce agents to negotiate for given goods or services. These would include new communicative acts, to allow negotiation to be effectively conducted to the satisfaction of all parties involved.
- **Financial management.** This includes tools and technologies to cover aspects of charging for goods (including billing and maintaining accounts), electronic payment, and general accounting practices in the country of origin.
- **Authentication.** An important necessary (though not sufficient) first step is to be able to authenticate the identity of both seller and buyer agents, and the users or organizations they represent.
- **Nonrepudiation.** Nonrepudiation mechanisms ensure that deals are made in such a way that they can be enforced or that there is redress for the injured party if the deal fails after being agreed on. This may have implications for international law.
- **Representation of goods and services.** To be able to trade in a market for a given good, agents must be able to represent that good. The market must be fair and accurate and avoid misrepresentations.
- **Market mechanisms.** For agents to be able to trade with each other, there must be markets where they can gain the necessary knowledge of the goods available, promote their goods, and strike deals. Especially in the case of open markets, buyer and seller agents must be able to enter, trade, and exit the market in a fixed way.
- **Identification.** The agent must be able to identify sites that offer the goods and services that it seeks.

## THE FUTURE

The future for online shopping is very dynamic and will remain that way. Vendors are continually looking for technologies similar to agents to boost sales. Retail management will be delighted at the prospect of reducing expensive overhead of inventory and will switch to the just-in time Internet-based type of sales. But old-style bricks and mortar stores and strip malls will not become a distant memory. Some customers still have to have the touch and feel of a product or fabric or see the real color or smell the perfume. But they can still order online and confirm their order by visiting the nearest store and picking up the order if it passes the touch and feel test. Agent technology will become an enablement helping consumers by suggesting the best prices, alerting then when something comes into stock, and inventively performing a myriad of other tasks that we have not yet thought about.

# CHAPTER

## 15

# Media

*Any technology that disseminates news, imagery to the people is very very useful.*

—His Holiness, the Dalai Lama

Agents are rapidly becoming a major part of news and entertainment systems, both in-house and externally through the Internet and other interfaces. Media businesses have been quick to see the potential, and there are many examples of first-generation computer agents in this field. The media world is quite broad, covering newspapers, television, movies, music, games, magazines, and entertainment centers such as Disney. Media companies were early adopters of the Internet.

By 1995, many U.K. and U.S. newspapers had online versions. The online versions were, in most cases, straight copies of the text paper, usually a subset of stories, almost a come-on for the "'real" newspaper. Many more have come online during the last three years, so that now almost every newspaper has an Internet presence.

Hollywood and other film media centers have also been early adopters, using the Internet to promote new films by offering "inside" news, interviews with stars, and still pictures. In a similar fashion, the music industry has well-known sites profiling groups and their albums.

TV stations, particularly cable stations, have been quick to exploit another medium. CNN Interactive is a classic case of using the choice power of the Internet to offer in-depth coverage and a wider range of stories.

The media business in general has invested recently in "push" technologies, and online magazines have sprung up to bring subscribers regular editions of such famous magazines as *Elle*. The main news magazines such as *Time* and *Newsweek* have not followed suit (maybe because the paper version offers little value to an Internet publication).

The most famous example of push technology in this area is Pointcast, which in 1996 began a news delivery system that was unique and offered a wide range of news and entertainment. Information of every conceivable type is delivered automatically to your desk when you log on, or if on a corporate system, in real time. The data is also displayed as a screen saver with news, stocks, weather, and other data flying across a screen.

Several upstream news companies (traditionally providers to other news media) have begun to push down-market into the consumer domain. Reuters and Dow Jones both offer news systems on the Internet.

The accompanying examples show service offerings of some of these companies.

*USA Today* uses an agent called Swoop to assist job seekers by e-mailing them when it locates jobs that match their requirements and allows them to view company details if they are interested in applying.

Agents are springing up to identify advertisements in the job, housing, and auto markets and to let the online reader find the advert for the item being sought. For regional press, these agents will help differentiate offerings.

Newspapers, magazines, and TV companies have so far failed to discover a new role on the Internet, and this failure has inhibited agent development (if you don't know what you are, you cannot effectively develop ancillary services).

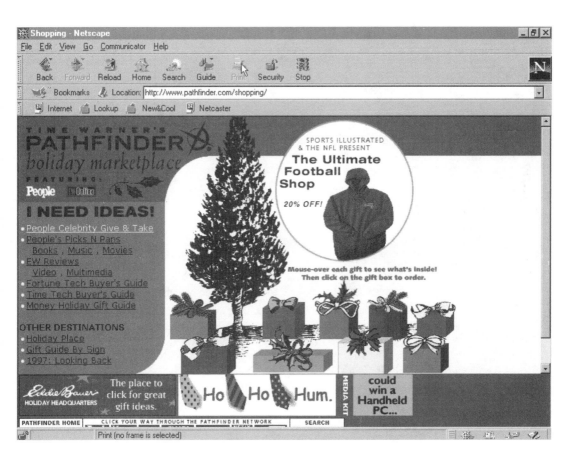

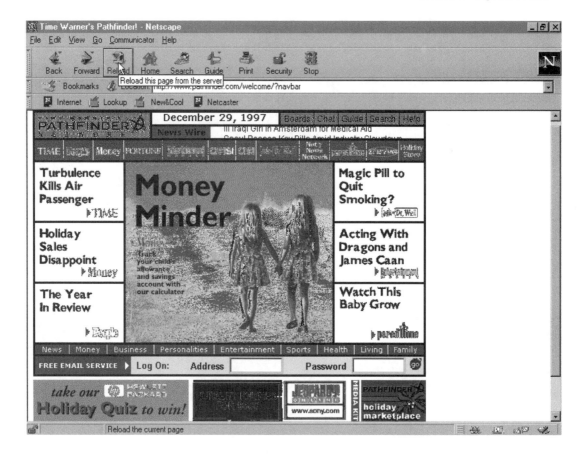

## AGENTS IN THE PRODUCTION PROCESSES

The initial glitter of Web presence has begun to die down, and media companies are now looking at the Internet as a means of working with customers and improving production.

The main areas where the use of the Internet is helpful is as follows:

*Eliminating "special" communications technology for delivering copy.* Copy delivery has been a nightmare for international papers and wires. Every country has varied communications methods; however, the Internet finally provides a level playing field.

*Electronic links with suppliers and customers.* This is a wide-ranging use. Newspapers, for example, want to know from the major distributors what last night's sales were as quickly as possible. Also, the adverts are usually placed by agencies, and copy is handled in most newspapers manually.

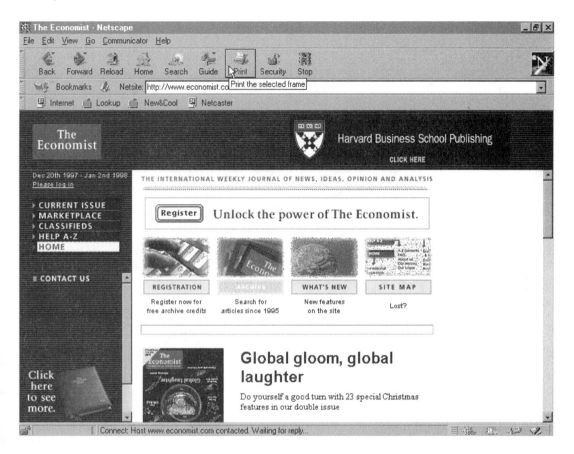

Agents could be employed in this process to ensure that copy from outside sources arrives, and if it does not, to substitute house ads.

Most major newspapers are now investigating how to use computer agents to assist in these areas. A good example is a product from Mediamatic SA in Sweden. This uses a combination of local Java applets on a browser and server side agents to allow large users of classified advertising (such as property, jobs, and automobiles) to enter their own adverts using a browser on the Internet and actually to see the copy as it will appear in the paper. This process is done by the agent, which picks up the incoming copy, passes it through Quark Express (the page assembly tool), and returns to the client a GIF image of this advert. This use of agents is set to explode as it creates a win-win situation. The advertiser feels more in control of copy, and the paper saves staff time.

Agents are also used by Web versions of newspapers to "tailor" copy to a client's request. A few intrepid newspapers, such as the *Washington Post* and *New York Times,* and magazines such as the *Economist* have begun to charge for Web

access. One of the benefits offered is that the Web subscribers get exactly what they want. A combination of user profiles and agents provides this service. At the *New York Times* with some 300,000 clients, the supporting hardware and software to provide this function is massive.

## Summary

The conclusions from this assessment are interesting. We see agent technology as a significant enablement factor in making media interests more personalized and interactive and ultimately more profitable. It can help with the filtering of information so that the user gets

> The right information
> In the right time frame
> In the right format

At the right price
At the right volume and quantity
At the right style and approach.

Where else is there an approach that will provide all these factors? Agents are the answer.

# 16

# Agents in Information Technology (IT)

## CORPORATE NETWORKS

Corporate computer networks are the absolute lifeblood of the modern corporation. They are the main arteries of information, data, voice, e-mail, fax, and now the Internet that allows business to communicate both internally and with the outside world. Corporations both large and small cannot function effectively without huge networks. They have complicated technical architectures beyond the comprehension of most employees. But try conducting business without such a network. Corporations are now very dependent on having fast, reliable, and accessible networks twenty-four hours a day, seven days a week, fifty-two weeks a year.

But business growth and applications developers are creating unprecedented levels of network demand. One of the most basic and dominant factors contributing to this growth in demand for all aspects of networking emanates from the steady and sustained overall growth in the economy. Organizations are continuing to report record revenue and earnings while unemployment is at its lowest levels in three decades, stimulating a buoyant economy and trade.

This sustained favorable business climate has led to business expansion, mergers, acquisitions, new market ventures with existing products and services, and diversification into new product or service areas. During this multiyear period of business growth, we have seen how business growth, expansion, and diversification almost always leads to an overall increased demand for IT services. In particular, there is a profound increase in demand for networking professionals to plan, design, implement, and operate networking hardware, software, and services solutions so vital to continue this growth.

Managing these vital networks is important to their growth and the profitability of parent organizations, and they now need sophisticated tools for maintaining and managing. Some organizations are leading the way with agent technology. Agents now routinely provide many management services for controlling these vastly complex architectures, data, and volumes, including the following:

- Monitoring to service levels agreements (SLAs) and scheduled collection of information, volumes, and data
- Determining threshold exceptions
- Forwarding event information with recommendations to network managers
- Executing recovery actions, and storing parameter and event information
- Providing selected metrics, files, and processes
- Acting as problem probes
- Changing hardware configuration
- Rerouting data, voice, video, e-mail when outages occur
- Gathering information (by polling) from all the other agents and having the "intelligence" to know what to do
- Finding alternate devices for printing, collating, faxing, or routing e-mail users, automatically without interruption of service

## NETWORK AGENT VENDORS

The market for agent software is rapidly expanding, and vendor interest is beginning to pick up. Listed in the table is a sample of products and vendors. Again, no one vendor dominates the market, and it is open to competition.

| Product | Vendor |
| --- | --- |
| TME 10 modules—Tivoli | IBM |
| IT/O Agent Openview | Hewlett Packard |
| Patrol Agents | BMC Group |
| TNG Agents | Computer Asociates |
| Bull ISM Agent Integrator | Groupe Bull |
| Command Center | Candle |
| Ecotools | Compuware |
| ProVision | Platinum Technology |

In the future, perhaps within the next five years, we expect that an agent can act as a "superagent" that controls subagents (agent-to-agent integration). The superagent can make correlation of events from its subagents to perform some local action on the managed system. It takes control on the subagents according to some policy management already determined by network professionals. Network "war rooms" or planners to monitor real-time agent activities will also use three-dimensional virtual reality cockpits.

Corporations seeking continuance of growth and excellence must actively involve agents in the management of advanced networks and selectively apply advanced technologies at the strategic planning, tactical planning, and operational execution levels. They are extremely complex now and are growing in sophistication and volume, and will need technologies such as agents to maintain and control that growth.

# CHAPTER

## 17

# Government

## SPACE EXPLORATION

Space—the final frontier—is the last great exploring adventure that awaits us. However, because of the size, nature, and vastness of space there are some basic fundamental problems that must be solved. The successful exploration of space will require a large number of cheap, agile, and smart spacecraft that can undertake ambitious mission to the far corners of the universe.

To achieve this goal requires that spacecraft will be very different from the vehicles that we have developed over the last thirty years. It will require spacecraft that are independent, autonomous, and smart. They must be capable of solving problems without human intervention. In the past, spacecraft needed great numbers of staff to carry out all the necessary functions to design, launch, track, manage, retrieve, and then interpret the data or results.

This approach is no longer viable or acceptable because of a number of factors.

1. Space is immense and requires traveling huge distances.
2. Previous missions have been very expensive. Now the drive is towards "better, cheaper, faster."
3. Large-scale automation is necessary for deep-space exploration. Automation implies sophisticated software.
4. Humans cannot endure multiyear space flights, and there is a requirement for unmanned missions.

To engage this approach, organizations such as NASA have been developing numerous agent-based technologies that will address many of these issues. NASA's New Millennium Project (NMP) is one such example. It is the first agent-based software in combination with other artificial intelligence software that will completely control a space exploration mission. It will accelerate the infusion of technologies into its space and Earth science missions of the twenty-first century. The program plans a series of technology-validation flights in the 1998–2000 time frame, anticipating a rate of two flights per year, which will demonstrate that technologies for deep-space and Earth-orbiting missions will work successfully. In tandem with developing and validating new technologies, NMP is also undertaking new management approaches, particularly in the area of partnering between government and industry. A novel application of the concept of integrated product development teams (IPDTs) is being pursued: one in which cross-organizational teams, made up of members from government, industry, and academia, create roadmaps for development of the high-payoff technologies such as agent technology that NMP intends to validate with flights. The IPDT approach is expected to reduce costs and improve product. These are examples of the management challenges that must be addressed today in order more efficiently to undertake space exploration and Earth observation in the twenty-first century: the new millennium.

## How Does It Compare?

The following comparison will give some perspective on how much taxpayer money is being spent to accomplish these extraordinary goals in space exploration—and ultimately to enhance mankind's understanding of the universe we live in:

> The budget for the movie *Titanic* was over $200 million, which was more than the budget for the first DS1 mission ($139.5 million), which will fly by an asteroid and return information on the kind of celestial body that might once have slammed into Earth. DS1 will also fly by a comet and take pictures and measurements of its tail, gathering information that might give scientists clues to the origins of the solar system—all for less than the cost of a single Hollywood movie.

NASA is preparing the most advanced spacecraft artificial intelligence software yet developed for launch aboard the Deep Space One (DS 1) spacecraft.

## The First Deep Space One (DS1) Mission

In Chapter One of this book, we referred to the HAL 9000 main computer, which can be compared with the future generation of agent technology. According to the book "2001," by Arthur C. Clarke, HAL "became operational" on January 12, 1997, in Urbana, Illinois home of the University of Illinois. It then served as the "brain and nervous system" of the 400-foot-long spaceship *Discovery* that carried astronauts on a thought-provoking voyage to the planet Saturn (changed to Jupiter in the movie version).

The robotic DS1 spacecraft carries no crew and is much smaller than the fictional spaceship of *2001*, at a total mass of 945 pounds, but its computer artificial intelligence program, known as the Remote Agent, shares the same basic goal of operating and controlling a spacecraft with minimal human assistance. The software will logically reason about the state of the spacecraft, and the Remote Agent will consider all the consequences of its actions.

**The Deep Space 1 craft looks like a normal spacecraft—but it's completely self-sufficient and autonomous because of agent technology.**

Following its scheduled 1998 launch, DS 1 will fly by the asteroid McAuliffe (named after the teacher Christy McAuliffe, who perished in the Challenger Shuttle disaster in 1985) and then continue by the comet West-Kohoutek-Ikemura and the planet Mars in 2000. DS 1 is the first scheduled mission in NASA's New Millennium program. The Remote Agent is being developed in a collaborative effort between NASA Ames and the Jet Propulsion Laboratory (JPL), Pasadena, California.

The Remote Agent should enable future spacecraft software to be designed more easily. The first version of Remote Agent will be the hardest and most difficult to write. After that, it can then be copied for the next mission and improvements made in it rather than software having to be developed from scratch. It will be continuously improved with knowledge gained from each mission.

This procedure is made possible by model-driven software. Models of the spacecraft's components and environment are given to the Remote Agent, and it figures out the necessary detailed operating procedures on its own. Only the models need to be updated for each new spacecraft.

Because of NASA's continuing efforts to develop many smaller, less expensive science spacecraft, each mission with fewer than a dozen ground controllers may be carried out instead of the hundreds of people now needed to run a major planetary science mission. The large distances inherent in planetary exploration cause communications to be too slow to be acceptable during normal operations and unacceptable during emergencies. Even signals from nearby planets such as Mars take eleven minutes to be received, and sometimes the communication pathway is blocked when a planet is between the spacecraft and Earth.

Three parts of Remote Agent will work together to demonstrate that it can autonomously operate a spacecraft: High Level Planning and Scheduling, Model-based Fault Protection (also called Livingstone, named after the nineteenth-century medical missionary and African explorer), and Smart Executive (see the accompanying figure).

Some estimates show a 60 percent reduction in mission costs by using the Remote Agent. The software would replace a large section of the human spacecraft control team back on Earth.

The High Level Planning and Scheduling part of Remote Agent will constantly look ahead to the schedule for several weeks of mission activities. Planner is mostly concerned about scheduling spacecraft activities and distributing resources such as electrical power. The Planner allows a small spacecraft control team on Earth to command the spacecraft more effectively by sending goals instead of detailed instructions to DS 1.

After DS, NASA intends to work on even more autonomous spacecraft that could reconfigure themselves. If some part of such a spacecraft performed differ-

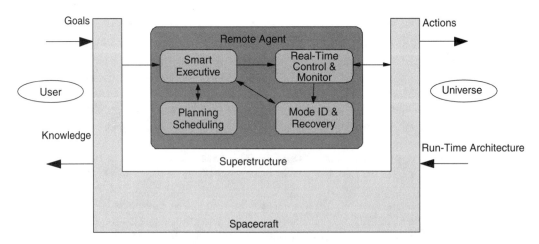

**Architecture Diagram of the DS Remote Agent Technology**

ently than expected during the mission, the craft would be able to detect this difference and change software models and algorithms to self-adapt.

The fault protection portion of the Remote Agent, Livingstone functions as the mission's virtual chief engineer. If something should go wrong with the spacecraft, Livingstone would use the computer model of the way that the spacecraft should be behaving to diagnose failures and suggest recoveries.

The third part of the Remote Agent sofware, Smart Executive, will act like an executive officer of the mission, issuing general commands to fly DS1. The Executive has to be able to execute the plans that are produced by the Planner and Livingstone. If the Planner had to worry about every single detail, it would be hard-pressed to produce a plan. Therefore, the Executive takes care of the details.

The Executive also can receive a plan or single commands directly from ground controllers. However, if the ground's plan won't work, the Executive can say, "Sorry, Ground, I can't do that." This can actually be a big help to ground controllers, who must currently expend enormous effort double-checking every command and then not always getting it right. In a sense, Executing Agents can test different scenarios in real time.

In the event that the Remote Agent won't cooperate under some unusual circumstance, NASA will be developing a surgery mode with which ground control can really get into Remote Agent and take corrective action. Remote Agent may someday lead to software that would be incorporated into a space robot that would be as intelligent as HAL 9000.

*The New Millennium Program has accelerated technology development in agent-based spacecraft automation by at least ten years.* The Remote Agent will open up new exploration opportunities, allowing us to begin really the insitu era of space science. Future systems also should be able to learn about their environment and act in partnership with scientists to find and analyze new discoveries. The key issue for the program in the next few years will be to make it work successfully.

Looking ahead even further, NASA plans to build a fleet of these smart spacecraft, called spacecraft constellations or armadas, and to let them explore different places, share their findings, and even divide amongst themselves the work of achieving complex scientific goals. Systems like the Remote Agent will be crucial supporting components of this vision. For more information, visit The New Millennium Project

http://nmp.jpl.nasa.gov/

## AGENTS IN THE WHITE HOUSE

The President of the United States is a lightning rod for all types of correspondence. Each day, thousands of letters, faxes, telephone calls, and now e-mail arrive at the White House on every conceivable subject, concern, or request from citizens of the United States and people all over the world. With the explosion of the Internet, citizens can now easily e-mail the White House (President@white-house.gov), and we urge you to e-mail the President on all your concerns.

To manage this daily deluge and to maintain security, the White House Technology Unit installed an agent system to handle the growing amount of e-mail. The agent scans each message and matches subjects, then forwards it to the appropriate government department for action, (you hope); for example, if you were concerned about the situation in Bosnia, first your message will be acknowledged and then will be forwarded to the State Department. Like all good agent systems, it is customizable and flexible, so the White House staff can add events as they happen; for example, the staff might add "floods in the Midwest" in the spring or some exotic name of a city anywhere in the world that becomes news. When a message is sent, autoresponder sends back text to the originator.

> Thank you for writing to President Clinton via electronic mail. Since June 1993, the President has received over 2.3 million messages from people across the country and around the world. Online communication has become a tool to bring government and the people closer together.
>
> Because so many of you write, the President cannot personally review each message, though he does receive samples of his incoming correspondence. The White House Correspondence staff helps him read and respond to the mail. All responses are mailed via the U.S. Postal Service. This is the only electronic message you will receive from whitehouse.gov. No other message purporting to be from the President or his staff with an address at whitehouse.gov is authentic. If you have received such a message, you have received a "spoof."
>
> We appreciate your interest in the work of the Administration.
>
> Sincerely,
>
> Stephen K. Horn
> Director, Presidential E-mail
> The Office of Correspondence

However, not all of the e-mail is polite. The President regularly receives hate mail and threats on his life. All threats are taken very seriously. The agent checks messages for key words such as "kill," "eliminate," or "assassinate," as well as expletives that our publisher will not allow us to print, and directs those messages to the FBI for action. *The system is sophisticated enough to hunt down the authors of anonymous messages.* It traces backwards through servers and networks and the Internet, keeping track of where it has been—a kind of reverse messaging system. Several would-be assassins have been apprehended and interviewed. We attempted to get further information for this book, but our attempts were met with a "no comment."

The agent system is very effective. This Reuters news report 27th of January, 1997, illustrates just how effective.

**More than one type agent is in the White House.**

Two New Hampshire high school students are suspected of emailing a death threat to President Clinton.

The two 10th-graders were suspended from Profile High School here after the Secret Service said it had traced the email to the students. The email was sent January 13, Secret Service agent James Fitton said from his office in Concord, New Hampshire.

Bethlehem School Superintendent Robert Horan said the students claimed they never expected the message to reach the president. The email, which arrived at a White House Web site, was intercepted by the Secret Service and traced back to a Profile High computer lab.

The students were suspended until the end of the month and have been banned from logging on to the school's Internet computer server for the rest of their high school years.

Federal officials say they doubt criminal charges will be filed. "We're satisfied the school took appropriate action against the students," Fitton said.

The incident marks the third time Clinton has been threatened by email from New Hampshire students during the past three months, Fitton said. Two juveniles from Keene and Salem also made such threats, Fitton said.

So watch what you say in your e-mail, and be polite to the President—unless you want a visit from the men in dark suits, wearing sunglasses and exhibiting bulging armpits and hearing aids.

CHAPTER

# 18

# Unusual Agents

## MARINE AGENTS IN A VIRTUAL AQUARIUM

One interesting and unusual application of agents can be found in the virtual aquarium. This is a software prototype system that is being tested in Darmstad, Germany, and will be used at various shows and exhibitions in Europe. The Franhofer Institute of Computer Graphics designed and created this software aquarium to simulate and to provide education about the fragile nature of the marine ecosystems.

It consists of a full marine aquarium complete with fish, sharks, crabs, dolphins, and other marine creatures, all designed by software. The agent fish—and there are over 3,000 of them in approximately 300 different species—interact with each other to simulate marine behavior in the real ocean by swimming, gathering in schools, hunting, feeding, and reacting to predators. Each marine creature is a mobile agent that is interacting with other agents around it.

A diver wearing a virtual reality helmet can explore the bottom of the virtual ocean and interact with the fish and other marine inhabitants without getting wet or going near the ocean.

Visitors can view the aquarium on a large movie-style screen and see what the diver sees. Additional realism is provided by sound effects such as air bubbling out of air tanks and other watery noises as the diver moves. Also, a variety of musical backgrounds create atmosphere and emotion, in the way that movie soundtracks do.

The system, which took two years to design and construct, consisted of a team of programmers, biologists, and marine scientists. The Franhofer Institute is a computer center that develops a wide variety of virtual reality software and includes other applications in numerous fields, such as:

- Modern architecture construction
- Aircraft design and flight simulation
- Urban planning
- Industrial manufacturing
- Car assembly and testing
- Reconstruction of historical sites

**Agent sharks and fish swim in the virtual Aquarium.**

- Medicine
- Entertainment and art

## THE VIRTUAL BOSTON SCROD

Another example of the virtual fishtank can be found nearer to home at the Boston Computer Museum in Massachusetts. Here again visitors to the museum can create their own virtual agent fish that interact with other species in a simulated marine environment.

This large exhibit, over 2,200 square feet, has been developed in collaboration with the nearby and famous MIT Media Lab, which has been developing pioneer multimedia applications and artificial intelligence applications for many years. A high-speed data network with twenty-four large capacity personal computers drive the large display consisting of twelve large back projection screens.

A "Build your Own" fish station allows visitors to construct a fish, tell it how to react, that is, timidly, aggressively, or passively and further to describe its personality. Then they can launch their creation into the virtual tank and observe its behavior with other fish and marine animals.

The whole system, which cost in excess of $1 million, will give hours of agent pleasure.

## VIRTUAL PETS

First introduced in Japan in November 1996, the first virtual pet was called a Tamagotchi (pronounced TAH-MAH-GOH-CHEE), which means "cute little egg," and sold in toy stores, and it was marketed as "the original virtual reality

**The first example of a consumer-based, handheld believable agent, which is approximately the same size as a key chain.**

pet." It is a tiny handheld, LCD video game with agent-based software that comes attached to a key chain or bracelet (see the accompanying illustration). The object of the game is to simulate the proper care and maintenance of a "virtual pet" such as a dog, cat, dinosaur, and many other types of pets with different personalities and temperaments. This is accomplished through performing the digital interaction of certain "parental" responsibilities, including many of the following:

- Feeding—Providing foods or milk
- Back—Calling the wandering pet back onto the screen
- Medicine—Giving injection shots for when it gets sick
- Spray—Spraying water at the pet agent
- Clean—Cleaning up the poop as for other pets
- Play—Learning that all pets like to play
- Catch—Catching the pet and moving it around
- How (status check)—Seeing what the pet needs when it calls you
- Games—Playing a game such as tennis with another pet
- Health—Reporting in depth on your pet's health and well-being
- Mute—Turning off the sound for about an hour
- Sleeping—Turning the light off
- Suspend—Setting on pause for the life cycle

This is an example of a "believable agent" that entertains and interacts on behalf of its owners. However, the manufacturer makes no mention of the term "agent" in its advertising or manufacturing documentation.

## A Phenomenon in the Making

Over six million units have been purchased in Japan alone since the toy's release, meaning that an estimated 4 percent of the nation's population owns an agent technology as a toy. Priced at a minimum of $16, stores have consistently sold out of the item, inspiring an entire market of Hong Kong and Taiwan based counterfeit toy manufacturing operations. Would-be owners camp out overnight at stores expecting new shipments the next day, and some consumers resort to purchasing the toy eggs from black-market dealers, at prices ranging from twenty to sixty times the store price. Enterprising crooks sell fraudulent rain check coupons that can supposedly be exchanged for one of the electronic toys when the next shipment arrives.

In a highly publicized recent incident in Japan, four high school boys bullied a schoolmate and stole his egg. Police employed several patrol cars and a helicopter in the pursuit of the juveniles, and eventually recovered the electronic toy and returned it to the rightful owner (one wonders at the cost of this operation).

After more than twelve months of the toys being on the market, the craze shows no signs of slowing. The Japanese department store Torbu received a shipment of 1,000 units, all that they were allowed in a week, and despite efforts to keep potential customers in the dark about shipping schedules (to avoid enormous lines and unruly behavior), the new stock sold out in forty-five minutes.

Bandai Co., the producer of Tamagotchi, arguably the most successful virtual pet, is running ads in major newspapers in Japan apologizing for its inability to meet with consumer demand. It is claiming that the popularity of the toy caught them unawares and that they are upgrading their production facility in China to 3 million units per month.

Critics suspect Bandai of intentionally undersupplying in order to increase consumer demand. If so, they're in good company: This is typical of the marketing hype of Japanese companies. By keeping supply tight for the Nintendo Entertainment System and it subsequent reincarnations (Super Nintendo, Game Boy, and the Nintendo 64), the Nintendo Co. was able to maintain high consumer interest, thus yielding legendary sales. It is a very questionable business practice, if not illegal.

After test-marketing the product in select California and Hawaii toy stores in the United States, Bandai made its first official shipments of the product to an anxious consumer public on May 1, 1997. Analyzing the sales in Japan, American stores placed preorders for 6 million units, promising as much as $80 million in possible sales. Within twenty four hours the FAO Schwartz flagship toy store in Manhattan sold out of its first shipment of 10,000 units. An armored Brinks truck delivered 3,000 Tamagotchis to the sister store in San Francisco, and these were gone within five hours. A huge black market has been created by charlatans charging exorbitant prices to parents who must have the toy at any price.

Schools all over the world have imposed bans of the pets in classrooms, and teachers have confiscated many pets. In an attempt to smooth out the problem,

Tamagotchi's maker, Bandai America Inc., recently began drawing attention to a pause option on its toy. One enterprising company in America, the Cape Cod Potato Chip company of Hyannis, Massachusetts, is offering another solution: an employee-staffed "Electronic Pet Daycare Center," where children can send their virtual pets for free baby-sitting during the school year.

## Virtual Pet Cemetery

The pets can die if they do not receive appropriate care. When it is all over and if the owner feels strongly about the pet, then this Web site is dedicated to all those loved ones that have gone to cyber heaven. If you wish to immortalize your own beloved pet in the tombs of cyber space for eternity, you can create your own tombstone, crypt, or vault, and place it in the Virtual Cemetery. To get to the Virtual Cemetery, contact the site at

http://www.urban.or.jp/home/tobikan3/hakae/

## Future Pets

The success of consumer products like the pet depends on the continuing ability of manufacturers to produce better, more attractive products with new features. Will these pets be around five years from now? Probably—but in many different forms and styles. At present the agent interface is crude graphics with no color, sound, or video. Therein lies its future, and it's parting to the personal computer.

# 19

# Personalization–
# The Web's Holy Grail

## INTRODUCTION

The Holy Grail or "killer application" of the Internet is for corporations to deliver pinpoint, surgically accurate content on a one-to-one basis, every time, up to date, accurate, and affordable. Corporations are developing sites that cater to individual tastes to turn transitory or casual browsers into loyal, happy customers who return time and time again, and spend or buy. "Personalization technology" is actually a catchall for several underlying software techniques that serve targeted content in real time on the basis of user inputs and predetermined rules. But products that promise personalized Web experiences at the click of a button have, up to now, fallen short of the mark. Agents will play a big part in making personalization a reality.

The majority of corporations cite establishing loyalty as the greatest benefits of personalization technology. To maintain consumer market share, two-thirds are capturing e-mail addresses to deliver tailored notifications using agents. When asked what they perceive the visitor benefits to be, senior management listed delivering relevant content, automation of many tasks, making the user feel special, and simplifying navigation. Vendor instability, very high implementation cost (often between $500,000 and $3 million) and a lack of integration with complementary technologies have limited the adoption of personalization to only aggressive, leading-edge type corporations.

There are some conclusions we can draw from personalization already:

- Personalization is still in its early infancy—we might call it the first-generation of products.
- Corporations that have started have begun to use simple registration forms and topic queries.
- Some privacy fears and deployment costs hinder personalization adoption.
- Future acceptance depends on agent technology.

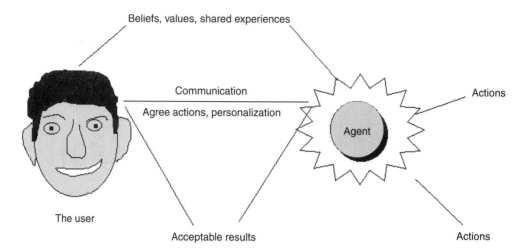

Beliefs, values, shared experiences

Communication

Agree actions, personalization

Agent

Actions

Actions

The user

Acceptable results

**Collaboration with Agents Leading to Personalization**

We can define this by referring to the accompanying figure.

### What Brings People Back to Your Web Site

According to a recent IntelliQuest survey, the top eight attributes that prompt Web customers to return to a Web site are as follows:

1. Very entertaining (56%)
2. Attention grabbing (54%)
3. Extremely useful content (53%)
4. Information tailored to a user's needs (45%)
5. Thought-provoking (39%)
6. Visually appealing (39%)
7. Imaginative (38%)
8. Highly interactive (36%)

Tailored Web information comes in at number four, which is very promising since personalization has not yet been adopted widely among Web developers and marketers. Industry analysts are predicting that the Web personalization technology will become a staple on Web sites in the next couple of years. Web personalization can increase the odds that people will come back to your site and spend more time perusing their personalized content versus aimlessly surfing for something that interests them. When it comes to the Web, users are looking for instant gratification and personalized information; therefore, offering personalized content is one way to meet this need.

### What Can Be Personalized?

Just about anything that is delivered through the Internet can be personalized and includes all categories of

- News—Local, international, special-interest
- Stocks—High risk, blue-chip, mutual fund
- Weather—In your state, in your country
- Music—What do you like?—classical, country, blues, rock, or reggae.
- Books—New releases, science fiction, hardbound, softcover
- Software—New releases, new products, upgrades
- Hardware—New announcements, printers, new models
- Sports—All types, results when they happen
- Newspapers—Getting a personalized copy of the *Wall Street Journal* or any other paper

Corporations too are beginning to understand the value of personalization and are delivering business content-specific information to users such as news: business news, breaking stories, mergers, interest rates, and alerts when a rate changes. Any business information can be distributed using this approach.

## CASE STUDY 1—ADVANCE BANK

The case study that we discussed in Chapter Thirteen is worth revisiting. This is the virtual bank created by Bayerische Vereinsbank (BV), the fourth largest bank in Germany, and Andersen Consulting worked together to create a virtual bank subsidiary called Advance Bank. The project's goal was to help the parent, BV, expand into untapped markets and outside country boundaries. One of the key factors in its success was *personalized service*. Customers have around-the-clock access to Advance Bank by phone, fax, PC, and the Internet twenty-four hours a day, seven days a week. Human interaction is always provided; therefore, Advance Bank is not using voice response units. In addition, 85 percent of the calls are answered in fifteen seconds. This high level of personalized service is key to helping Advance Bank capture expanded market share. In fact, the bank gained more assets in the first year than any other direct bank in Germany. It now intends to expand the level of service to provide automated personalization using agent technology over the Web.

## CASE STUDY 2—POINTCAST

Less than one year after PointCast launched its service in 1996 that automatically delivers news and information to screen savers of desktop computers, there has been an outpouring of interest in automated delivery technology (more commonly known as "push" and "netcasting") and its applications. This interest is primarily from workers within enterprises and from analysts, largely as a result of trade publications' and the mainstream national press's heralding the technology as the wave of the future. The following is a quote from their Web site:

> More than one million busy professionals rely on PointCast—the Internet's #1 news and information service. It's like having your very own personal assistant . . . someone to take care of gathering all the information you want to know and then presenting it to you on a silver platter. With PointCast, you get the news you need to stay on top—effortlessly. Information geared to your needs, personalized to your interests.
>
> No purchase price, no monthly fees, no kidding.
>
> Get local, national, and international news; stock information; industry updates; weather reports; sports scores and more from leading sources like CNN, The Wall Street Journal and The New York Times—all integrated in a personalized, easy-to-digest newscast.

Pointcast is at
http://www.pointcast.com

Other examples that have been announced in the past eighteen months include Netscape (Netcaster), Microsoft (Active Channels), and BackWeb (Marimba).

**Pointcast—the very successful personalization assistant delivering news, stocks, sports, and other information to over a million users.**

## TYPES OF TECHNOLOGY

There are seven technologies associated with personalization.

1. *Cookies and certificates:* These require identification by the user with data stored in the PC client or host and matching the profiles.
2. *Neural nets:* These analyze user logs offline and user click stream data online to identify behavioral patterns. These patterns can then be used to predict in real time what content will be most relevant to a particular user.
3. *Collaborative filtering applications:* These determine clusters of users with similar interests, either by asking users explicitly or by using business rules to determine those interests implicitly. **Uses agent technology.**
4. *Rules-based applications:* These use human-determined rules to select classified content on the basis of user behavior. **Uses agent technology.**
5. *Electronic catalogs:* These present a customized view of a catalog to a buyer on the basis of that buyer's explicit preferences and historical profile. **Uses agent technology.**
6. *Configuration engines:* These use a series of pre-defined questions to route an end user through a complex product or service selection process. **Uses agent technology.**
7. *Personalized e-mail.* This method provides customized editorial or promotional information by e-mailing it directly to customers. It is a low-cost "push" application that enables you to provide information, even multimedia, via e-mail. The e-mails can also serve as periodic reminders to your customers to visit your Web site. **Uses agent technology.**

### Privacy

An important and hotly debated issue is privacy. What makes personalization valuable to Web users also makes users uneasy: providing personal information. Users have historically been uneasy about giving personal information to anyone. Successful implementations of Web site personalization involve educating the customer about the benefits of providing personal information and keeping this information confidential, and also, giving the user the choice of keeping the information private or allowing Web marketers to pass along their information, such as e-mail and physical addresses, to other companies. Etrust (http://www.etrust.org) is one organization that is establishing guidelines for data privacy and security where Web sites can display "Trustmarks" based on levels of data exchange between the user and the Web site and/or third-party organizations. Etrust's mission is to increase trust through the disclosure of data-gathering practices by the Web merchant to Web users. Other such systems will evolve until the marketplace accepts a standard.

## WHO ARE THE PLAYERS?

The following vendors may be classed as Tier 1, or the first to enter the market-place.

| Vendor | Product |
| --- | --- |
| Firefly Network | Catalog Navigator |
| | Firefly Passport Office |
| Gustos Software | Gustos Guide |
| Like Minds, Inc. | Preference Server |
| Net Perceptions, Inc. | Grouplens |
| Wisewire | Wisewire for Websites |
| Brightware, Inc. | Brightware |
| Multilogic | Selector |
| PersonalLogic, Inc. | PersonalLogic |
| Affinicast, Inc. | Affinicast Marketing |
| Autonomy, Inc. | AgentWare |
| Broadvision | One on One and others |
| GuestTrack, Inc. | Guestrack |
| Micromass | Intelliweb |
| Open Sesame, Inc. | Open Sesame |
| Microsoft, Inc. | Site Server |

We regard the following as major market players: Microsoft, Broadvision, Firefly, Likeminds, and NetPerceptions.

## CONCLUSIONS

We predict that in the next few years, as personalization evolves and matures, that "individual pages will be matched to individual interests with a precision not seen before." And the result may be unnerving, as marketers start using the Internet as an instrument to peer not just into the habits but into even the thought processes of individual computer users. We also expect the major change in electronic commerce to be driven by the successors to the personalization technology. Such changes are now being incorporated into Web servers, tools, and databases. The new systems are expected to collect a wider range of information, such as sequence of pages and sites visited, including time spent at each page. For example, banks will monitor how long users stay on a mortgage site and then send them applications for a mortgage. Such information will be stored in databases, and marketers will tap into this vast database for consumer information.

As a user signs on in the future, information from the database will be retrieved to target specific information about the individual. According to Larry Footer, Chief Executive Officer of Consortium LLC, a New York–based Internet software developer: "Selling on the Internet no longer will be based on demographics. It's all psychographics. You want to know what a consumer is thinking." He also said that small merchants will use existing data to determine whether to offer premium or discount items to particular online customers.

The Chief Executive Officer of the successful personalization online bookseller, Amazon Books, Jeff Bezos, predicts that Web retailing will never replace traditional retail shopping, but consumers may be inclined to shop online if more companies were to offer personalized content and services. He said, "The potential is there to completely redecorate your storefront for every customer that comes to your site." Nevertheless, he considers the development of this technology to be necessary for long-term survival. We believe he is right, and we support his view. Furthermore, customized content may not be completely viable until the technology becomes more accessible and is easier to implement. It can also be very expensive, so that there is a case here for quantum drops in costs. "If it's cheap, they will come."

# 20

# New Opportunities

## SECOND-GENERATION WEB SITES

If we examine the development of the Internet, it is clear that an evolution is taking place, which is driven by the growing capability of computer agents. What is developing is the second-generation Web site. This is a Web site that has no content of its own but that acts as an integrator of other Web sites in a particular field.

Examples abound and are of varied sophistication. Pointcast, Insight, and others have created very general environments, which a customer can tailor to provide news, entertainment, and other information to her or his personal liking. These are very sophisticated systems integrating other information sources under license.

But in many other areas, of which the most developed is probably sex sites, whole webs are really just pointers to other webs. Persian kitty is an example of a web site that provides this service. It checks information such as registration required, content, costs, and delivers to the owner. By offering this kind of site, Internet hosts are mirroring the development of newspapers in the early part of the century when wire services provided an editor with access to stories from all over the world, which he or she would sift, and then the editor would deliver to his or her clients what seemed relevant to them.

The big difference with computer agents is that the agents go looking, rather than waiting for delivery. This process potentially cuts out the role of the human agency. Let's take news as an example. Reuters and Dow Jones make their money (and it is big money—they are two of the largest companies in the world) by acting as the agents of delivery for news stories actually gathered by some thousands of on-the-street journalists around the world. The value of these agencies was providing the network of relationships and technology that delivered those stories rapidly to a central office and the network that delivered them to customers all over the world.

Today we are not very far from the reporter's having a digital camera in the field, which is connected by cellular network to her or his Web page. As the reporter speaks and writes (using a palm PC), these words are also appearing live on the Web. An intelligent agent from any newspaper could (and we believe will) poll the Web pages as one of a group of "top" gatherers; determine whether the story is relevant or newsworthy enough; and if so, negotiate a price with the reporter's own negotiating agent; pull the story and/or pictures and voice; and credit the reporter's account automatically. Of course, the same agent would deliver the story to the page assembly agent, who would place the story on the right page according to its importance.

## OTHER EXAMPLES OF NEW OPPORTUNITIES

### Examples of Business Applications

- A dating service develops a Web-based package that allows customers to search for potential dating partners. A customer creates a personal agent and gives the agent his name, picture, and personal preferences. The agent then locates and communicates with other agents that represent possible partners.

- A car manufacturer implements a system that continually monitors cars for signs of trouble via a monitor agent in each of the manufacturer's cars. If the monitor agent detects a problem, the agent sends Java code to the manufacturer's home base via cellular and satellite networks indicating a problem. In response, the home base sends a copy of the latest diagnostic agent into the car. The diagnostic agent locates the problem, then collaborates with the manufacturer's scheduling agent and the car owner's personal agent to schedule the car for service at a suitable time. When all arrangements have been made, the car console display panel notifies the driver of the problem and recommends a course of action.

- A soft drink manufacturer creates a system that maintains a global network of 100,000 drink machines. By adding Java capabilities combined with pagerlike facilities to each machine, the manufacturer can refill and service the machines promptly. The manufacturer remotely deploys a monitor agent into each machine continually to check for low inventory and other problems. Updated versions of this agent are deployed as needed. If necessary, the drink prices are dynamically adjusted on a per-machine basis. In addition, marketing agents are deployed to conduct customer surveys and run focused marketing campaigns.

- An insurance company develops a policy system that evenly distributes the company's workload among many objects on multiple servers. An agent periodically measures the CPU load on each machine and accordingly moves the objects around at run time. When necessary, the agent copies these objects into work pools on remote servers.

- A telephone manufacturer develops Java-enabled cellular phones that help consumers find and purchase common items. Each cellular phone has a personal agent that proactively alerts the phone owner about movie tickets, plane tickets, videos, fast food, and other goods and services offered by a strategic set of leading vendors. The consumer appeal of this service results in a successful launch of the cellular phone, as well as in increased revenues for participating vendors.

# CHAPTER

$$\boxed{21}$$

# Avatars

## DEFINITION OF AVATARS

Avatars are computer representations of users in a computer-generated 3-D world. An avatar shows where a user is in the virtual world and which other users are in the same location. Advanced avatars can exhibit behaviors such as moods, voices, gestures, and facial expressions or "balloon-style" chat. An agent avatar can also be an automated "robot" with programmed behavior and responses.

As agents embody multiple knowledge representations—reasoning, decision, reaction, and learning capability—the goal is then to introduce believable emotions so that agents can gain some credibility. Avatars have been called the beginning of social computing. As more sophisticated interfaces close the gap between users and their machines and networks and as the Internet creates reliable links between these machines, users will face other communication challenges. The first challenge will be creating causality between the multiple agents, objects, and avatars. The consistent relationships existing between objects and their respective properties have to obey physical laws and commonsense behaviors. The advent of social computing will also bring a new set of communication ethical questions: Who will define the rules of interactions between agents and avatars, or for avatars among themselves? Who will define the code of ethics, standard behaviors, and the jurisprudence governing interactions among networks? How will standards incorporate all cultural sensibilities? Will developers rely on believable agents? What standards for avatars will evolve?

## THE DANCING BABY

The now famous Dancing Baby was "born" several years ago as Viewpoint model #VP5653—Toddler with Diaper. In 1996, Viewpoint provided the 3-D model to Kinetix for use as a Character Studio sample animation, and the Dancing Baby—a.k.a. Baby Cha-cha—evolved from that partnership. Since then, Dancing Baby has been embraced and customized by animators and graphics enthusiasts all over the world and everywhere on the Internet. He's even starred on several television network shows such as NBC, CNN, and CBS.

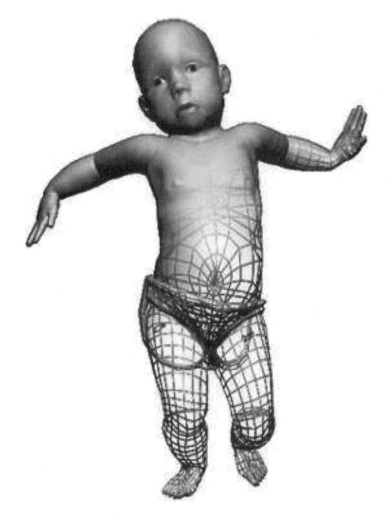

**The now-famous Dancing Baby.**

For example, military applications are pioneering many advances in the use of avatars. Sophistication in the virtual battlefield is such that trainees often cannot tell the difference between a human and a computer-generated avatar. Avatars have been used to introduce emotions such as fear and motivation in "enemy agents."

## RETAIL EXAMPLE

1. *Experiment:* In one experimental application, a retailer is using a robot avatar to sell vacuum cleaners. A softbot (that is, software agent robot) lis-

tens for certain keywords (mess, dirty, cleanup) in the chat room and zooms in to introduce itself to the user. It then attempts to sell the user a vacuum cleaner.

2. *Retail:* Sales is one of the most promising (as well as entertaining) areas for applications in the short term, that is, the next two years. It is possible to enhance online mail-order experiences by providing potential customers with innovative navigation means. By using their (truthful) measurements to generate an avatar to travel to an online mall, it will be possible for shoppers to have their virtual representations try on different items. They can choose different styles and change colors. From the individual to the collective experience, projected customers' personae could navigate virtual malls along with other avatars, adding a community dimension to the virtual shopping experience. This is a very ambitious undertaking, and we expect prototypes to be developed by leading agent software companies. Commercial applications will start to appear within 1999 to 2001. For those people who are overweight, perhaps a slimmer avatar will provide an impetus to lose weight: This is how you might look after losing thirty pounds?

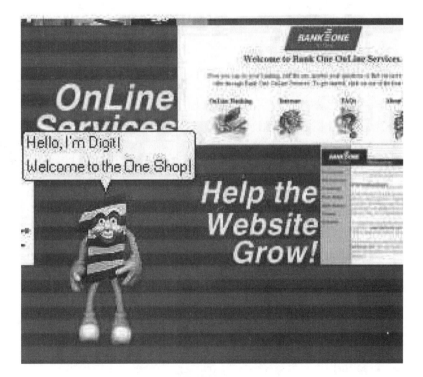

**This avatar appears on the desktop and can both speak and move around. It is one of the first avatars to be used in a banking environment.**

3. *Manufacturing:* Certain manufacturing industries are starting to take advantage of agents and avatars. Consider the space and the car manufacturing industries. Both have been an enabler of the most advanced technologies. Virtual reality and robotics are just a few examples. Avatars would add another dimension by allowing designers also to include themselves in the environments and thus to combine videoconferencing meetings and design collaboration sessions. The car industry could then use software avatars instead of crash dummies.

4. *Education:* Avatars have a great future in education, not merely acting as intelligent tutors but going beyond the rudimentary. Consider teaching languages as an example. Software could be created to produce an artificial world in the foreign country that is under study and to create avatars to speak and interact. Besides speaking, they could be dressed in the style of the country to add realism.

5. *Banking:* Bank One is the fifth biggest bank in the United States. Based in Columbus, Ohio, it has over 2,600 branches in 18 states, and it manages assets of over $350 billion. It has a large computer services organization with over 5,000 employees. Bank One introduced a Web presence in 1996 and has been experimenting internally with an avatar called "Digit" (after Bank One's name and logo).

## AGENTS AND AVATARS

The advent of personalizable avatars for which every user can customize her or his own avatar to explore interactive worlds and meet other participants is the dream of futuristic software companies. The ability to change the avatar type, size, gender, color, voice, accent, clothing, movements, and behaviors is desirable for success. Customizable but entirely flexible avatars are necessary to be accepted by the ever-demanding user. One minute the image of Marilyn Monroe, complete with curves, may be selected, and the next minute, a cute furry space alien with the voice of a three-year-old may be chosen.

Generating these characters by using tools such as Oz Character Creator™, which is a tool for creating AI-based believable characters, that have moods, likes, dislikes. This agent software is the main component of the Character Editor that controls the behavior of characters and allows users to communicate with them, whether they are in the 3-D world running in a Web page or a Java applet. The software uses complex parsing techniques to analyze user input and to configure appropriate answers. In addition to verbal responses, the characters can play back sound or video files and trigger predefined behaviors. The word lexicon containing 6,000 words can be easily customized. Words also have mood parameters that can be customized to generate a range of responses depending on the context and the mood of the character. A full-blown AI-based believable character, complete with family history, background, and purpose is included to illustrate the approach to creating the believable agents for the Internet.

## CONCLUSIONS

The combination of agents and avatars is an intoxicating mixture of future technology. However, there are the problems of acceptance and use before there can be success. Multimedia animation with voice and video quality requires heavy hardware configuration—at the moment—but as chip speeds become faster, this problem should subside. There is no question that certain well-designed and well-executed avatars will be useful in the right applications. Care should be taken not to make them too "cute" for business and commerce. People quickly get tired of repetition; as with screen savers, they want to change options frequently.

# The Future

CHAPTER

# 22

# The Next Decade

*The future ain't what it used to be.*

—Arthur C. Clarke

It is with some trepidation that we start this final section about the future of agent technology. It is commonplace that the future is inherently unknowable, unpredictable, and unreliable. Certainly, it is impossible to say with any precision what will be the course of future events. Nevertheless, we know something of the past and the present. From this, it is possible to construct models of the way that the world operates and from these to draw conclusions about the future.

The literature is crowded with futurology and forecasts on a whole range of subjects. Indeed, it has become something of an industry to be a forecasting futurist. These futurists can range from people who are attempting to provide a view of the world as a whole to researchers tracking a particular phenomenon (as we have attempted to do with agents). The approaches taken vary markedly. At one extreme, detailed mathematical models are constructed, while at the other, the author relies more on imagination and hypothesis. (We subscribe to both approaches.) There are also good forecasts and bad ones, and significantly there are gaps where few researchers have attempted to make projections.

As the following list shows, the past has been riddled with speculation.

## Amusing Examples of Technology Forecasting

"Computers in the future may weigh no more than 1.5 tons."
—*Popular Mechanics,* forecasting the relentless march of science, 1949

"I think there is a world market for maybe five computers."
—Thomas Watson, chairman of IBM, 1943

"I have traveled the length and breadth of this country and talked with the best people, and I can assure you that data processing is a fad that won't last out the year."
—The editor in charge of business books for Prentice Hall, 1957

"But what . . . is it good for?"

—Engineer at the Advanced Computing Systems Division of IBM, 1968, commenting on the microchip

"There is no reason anyone would want a computer in their home."

—Ken Olson, president, chairman, and founder of Digital Equipment Corp., 1977

"This 'telephone' has too many shortcomings to be seriously considered as a means of communication. The device is inherently of no value to us."

—Western Union internal memo, 1876

"The wireless music box has no imaginable commercial value. Who would pay for a message sent to nobody in particular?"

—David Sarnoff's associates in response to his urgings for investment in the radio in the 1920s

"The concept is interesting and well-formed, but in order to earn better than a 'C,' the idea must be feasible."

—A Yale University management professor in response to Fred Smith's paper proposing reliable overnight delivery service (Smith went on to found Federal Express Corp.)

"Who the hell wants to hear actors talk?"

—H. M. Warner, Warner Brothers, 1927

"I'm just glad it'll be Clark Gable who's falling on his face and not Gary Cooper."

—Gary Cooper on his decision not to take the leading role in *Gone With the Wind*

"A cookie store is a bad idea. Besides, the market research reports say America likes crispy cookies, not soft and chewy cookies like you make."

—Response to Debbi Fields's idea of starting Mrs. Fields' Cookies

"We don't like their sound, and guitar music is on the way out."

—Decca Recording Co., rejecting the Beatles, 1962

"Heavier-than-air flying machines are impossible."

—Lord Kelvin, president, Royal Society, 1895

"If I had thought about it, I wouldn't have done the experiment. The literature was full of examples that said you can't do this."

—Spencer Silver, on the work that led to the unique adhesives for 3M Post-It Notepads

"So we went to Atari and said, 'Hey, we've got this amazing thing, even built with some of your parts, and what do you think about funding us? Or we'll give it to you. We just want to do it. Pay our salary, we'll come work for you.' And they said, 'No.' So then we went to Hewlett-Packard, and they said, 'Hey, we don't need you. You haven't got through college yet.'"

—Apple Computer, Inc., founder Steve Jobs, on attempts to get Atari and HP interested in his and Steve Wozniak's personal computer

"Professor Goddard does not know the relation between action and reaction and the need to have something better than a vacuum against which to react. He seems to lack the basic knowledge ladled out daily in high schools."

—1921 *New York Times* editorial about Robert Goddard's revolutionary rocket work

"Can't act, can't sing, slightly bald. Can dance a little."

—Hollywood executive on Fred Astaire's first screen test.

"Drill for oil? You mean drill into the ground to try and find oil? You're crazy."

—Drillers whom Edwin L. Drake tried to enlist in his project to drill for oil in 1859

"Stocks have reached what looks like a permanently high plateau."

—Irving Fisher, Professor of Economics, Yale University, 1929

"Airplanes are interesting toys but of no military value."

—Maréchal Ferdinand Foch, Professor of Strategy, École Supérieure de la Guerre, France

"Everything that can be invented has been invented."

—Charles H. Duell, Commissioner, U.S. Office of Patents, 1899

"Louis Pasteur's theory of germs is ridiculous fiction."

—Pierre Pachet, Professor of Physiology at Toulouse, France, 1872

"The abdomen, the chest, and the brain will forever be shut from the intrusion of the wise and humane surgeon."

—Sir John Eric Ericksen, British surgeon, appointed Surgeon-Extraordinary to Queen Victoria, England, 1873

"640K ought to be enough for anybody."

—Bill Gates, commenting in 1981 on the amount necessary for computer memory requirements of the personal computer

"I have seen the future and it is very much like the present, only longer."

—Kehlog Albran, *The Profit*

"A good forecaster is not smarter than everyone else, he merely has his ignorance better organized."

—Anonymous

"To expect the unexpected shows a thoroughly modern intellect."

—Oscar Wilde

Now these three basic questions need to be addressed:

- What is the future for agent technology?
- What will that future look like?
- Who will be the major players?


## WHAT IS THE FUTURE FOR COMPUTERS AND THE INTERNET?

The accompanying illustration shows the likely development areas of the Internet over the next ten years.

### The Future of the Internet

| | | |
|---|---|---|
| Education delivery and management | News | TV Shows, movies entertainment |
| Research | | Gambling |
| E-Busines | | Employment |
| customer service | | |
| sales | | Voice and video communications |
| support | | Medicine and health |
| logistics mgmnt | | |

When we plot this against the likely areas of computer development over the same period

### Future of Computers

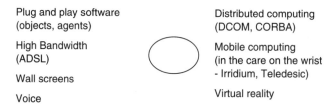

| | |
|---|---|
| Plug and play software (objects, agents) | Distributed computing (DCOM, CORBA) |
| High Bandwidth (ADSL) | Mobile computing (in the care on the wrist - Irridium, Teledesic) |
| Wall screens | |
| Voice | Virtual reality |

Then we must assume that agents are ready for a major takeoff. If we then look at the Internet itself and see that Internet 2 (or IPV6bone) plus HTML is being replaced by XML in the short term and VRML in the longer view, we perceive another set of convergences. These convergences all surround the ability of Web sites now and in the future to be responsive to agents and to provide an environment in which agents will thrive.

We have pointed to virus technology as being the forerunner (albeit a nasty one) of roaming agents. A real virus needs a culture into which it can fit and thrive. Currently, computer viruses are seen as a threat, and the "culture" we provide with Dr. Solomon and other virus catchers is pretty unfriendly. Perhaps the lasting achievement of virus attacks will be the healthy conservatism of software designers who will ensure that the space for agents to work in is safe and secure.

We cannot continue to use the Internet in the way that we are now doing. It is only the amazing excitement of this global entity that keeps us sitting for hours at our screens attempting, often unsuccessfully, to do real work. During the course of writing this book, we have often spent hours tracking down one simple fact. This is one area that agents will impact massively by being intelligent enough to absorb a need and to continue to search until the need is fulfilled. Another is in e-business, where agents will begin to replace people at a frightening rate in the very service industries to which we are looking for our future economy.

## WHAT IS THE FUTURE FOR AGENT TECHNOLOGY?

In general, we can sum up that future in one world—good. Clearly, as we have seen throughout this book, help is needed to deal with the ever-increasing digital deluge that we are subjected to. We see no need for agents to disappear or be replaced in the hype of any new technology. Quite the reverse. Agent technology will continue to be integrated into the Internet with increasing intelligence and sophistication.

Some predictions regarding agents technology are discussed in the following sections.

### Wearable Computers

Currently, there is a good deal of serious research being carried out at prestigious institutes such as IBM, Xerox, and MIT, in the area of wearable computers. A self-contained computer that is worn as a part of clothing is an intriguing possibility and has all the applications available from the normal desktop PC. It gives a whole new meaning to the term *mobile computing*. This is yet another trend towards integrating the computer in every aspect of our life and environment. The era of "smart clothes" is almost upon us. The wearable computer will need to be fundamentally different, lighter, faster, and nonintrusive, and have entirely different interfaces than what we are used to at present.

Wearable computers have been under development since the 1970s and have benefited from the quantum leaps in processor speed, communications, and software. Now with the Internet and many other advances, we see widespread practical acceptance of such technology as soon as it is comfortable to wear and use, cheap enough, and readily available.

The applications of agents in wearable/smart clothes will include many of the following:

1. Communication with the Internet, filtering, searching, formatting information and knowledge

This current example of the WearComp/WearCam invention comprises a complete multimedia computer, with camera, microphones, and earphones, all built into an ordinary pair of sunglasses except for some of the electronic items sewn into the clothing. Agents will be used to communicate, control, and disseminate information. Anyone want to buy one?

2. Operating system control, coordinating all input/outputs: voice, video, sounds, and so on
3. Security, protecting the wearer's information
4. Privacy, maintaining and protecting all data
5. Interacting with the wearer's other computers, desktops, laptops, by sending and receiving data

Clothing-based computing will blur the boundaries between seeing and viewing and between remembering and recording. Rather than narrowing our focus, living within our own personal information domain will enlarge our scope through shared visual memory that enables us to "remember" something or someone we may have never seen—for example, a brilliant sunset that we wish to remember from a vacation or photographs of people we have met, and so on. Agents are a natural technology to complement the wearable computer and to conduct the many activities we need to accomplish while on the move.

With a computer as close as the shirt on our back, interaction will become more natural. This will improve our ability to do traditional computing tasks while standing or walking, or even perhaps jogging, letting future computing systems function much like a second brain. A computer that is constantly attentive to our environment may develop situational awareness, perceptual intelligence, and an ability to see from the wearer's perspective and thereby assist in day-to-day activities.

These far-reaching goals will require five to ten years of more research. Nevertheless, we expect entirely new modes of human-computer interaction to arise, along with a whole new set of technical, scientific, and social needs that will have to be addressed as we take our first steps toward personal automation. Agents will continue to play an important and significant part of the development of this technology. We see agents as the "Technological Super Glue" that brings all the components of wearable computing together and make it work.

## E-Business

Agents will form the backbone of a e-business, which by its nature is twenty-four hours a day, seven days a week, fifty-two weeks a year. Agents will continue to spread up the value chain, gradually taking over many decision areas that are currently the domain of people. To achieve this, the esoteric arts of knowledge engineering will have to be transposed into simple technology, as is already happening with neural nets.

The example given earlier in the book of an automated customer service agent will rapidly become the norm, and the more advanced agents will, in fact, respond to a gradually increasing percentage of requests. This use will spread into the supplier chain, and agents on production lines will assess the need for product and then order it from supplier agents, negotiating price and delivery on behalf of their owners.

## Computer and Network Operations

There is a big opportunity area here for agents. Almost all companies are struggling with the personal computer cost equation. Masterful consultants chant the words "total cost of ownership (TCO)," and kimono-clad charismatic but misguided industry "leaders" invest shareholders' hard-earned money in "thin clients" and lose all the wealth built through years of struggle.

A large portion of the total cost of ownership (some 30 percent according to the analysts) is in day-to-day support. In most cases, a not very intelligent agent could solve the majority of these problems immediately. A large worldwide pharmaceutical company has 400 staff members around the globe doing help-desk support for its 50,000 staff members, and that is only for one software package SAP! The head of the operation told me that 90 percent of the calls concern simple items of understanding. How long will those 400 staff hold out in the agent society? At approximately $30,000 a head, that is $12 million per annum, not counting the buildings and phone costs. Probable cost is in the order of $25 million per annum when training and overall staff costs are taken into account.

You can get an awful lot of agent for $25 million, and the agent will run for years with no pay and no space.

If we then look at the global support business for software, we see a $25 billion per annum area. As most of the software in the world is becoming standardized on just a handful of packages, it is immediately clear that this area which employs some one million plus staff is ripe for downsizing in a big way, and it will be agents that will lead the way.

## THE AGE OF THE VIRTUAL CORPORATION

Five years in the future, the global corporate landscape will be totally different from that of today. Unless corporations adapt quickly—change, adapt, and most of all move rapidly to align with the constant changing market needs—then the horizon will be littered with the carcasses of failed corporations or enterprises that produce average mediocre products or services.

There has been much discussion about the virtual enterprise, and we need to review this at the end of our book, because we believe that it will be a dominant trend in future business. The economy of the future, driven by the constant formation and dissolution of thousands of virtual corporations, would be an economy dominated by more, but smaller, businesses that do one thing well and contribute that core expertise to numerous virtual enterprises, each of which makes and sells products that are good.

We may define the virtual corporation as "a legal enterprise or corporation that conducts business providing services, products, or other goods with little or no physical presence (bricks and mortar) and has a set of strategic alliances with other business entities, partnerships, and outsourced business processes other than its set of core specifics." The term *virtual* means "relating to something that appears to exist when in fact, it does not."

The virtual corporation approaches business in a new and fundamental way with

1. Heavy and continuous generation, and then exploitation of its own knowledge capital and intellectual property
2. Strong emphasis on fast multitiered telecommunications
3. Reliance on the Internet, internal networks, and intranets\extranets
4. Highly mobile and distributed knowledge or virtual employees
5. Horizontal, vertical, and functional teams of people accomplishing specific processes
6. Logical and flexible, rather than physical, structure
7. Very rapid product development (days and hours) and fast distribution deployment to waiting markets
8. Heavy emphasis on support, quality, and convenience
9. The development of integrated human and technological potential

Faced with this very agile competitor that will go to almost any length to gain market share, corporations will clearly have to identify key differentiators that can give the important competitive intelligence needed to make future profits. These organizations will have many existing and new tools to use such as

- Intranet/Extranet
- Electronic workplace overview and commentary
- Electronic workplace architecture and design
- Business intelligence
- Document imaging
- Electronic forms
- Intelligent agents
- Electronic mail and messaging
- Integrated documents management
- Information retrieval
- Knowledge management
- PC applications
- Intelligent documents
- Work flow and work management
- Workgroup systems and group ware

We predict that leading corporations will develop virtual intelligent agents (VIA's) that will be able to analyze, compile, and develop future products on the basis of data they find within the corporation. To achieve this, these highly mobile agents will perform a number of processes such as the following:

1. They will constantly scan and collect data all on their own internal processes, products, and services to identify new opportunities, new markets, potential threats, risks, and challenges.
2. They will sense changes in the global marketplace, with their suppliers, vendors, customers, clients, and competitors; adapt to changes made by regulators; and learn from the changes.
3. They will establish huge knowledge pools of products, in order to filter, interpret, and present data to management in new ways.
4. They will be an engine of continuous change, adapting and delivering quality products and services at lower cost/unit, and rapidly delivering what the market needs.

Clearly, as we have seen throughout this book, agent technology will **DOMINATE** this scenario. It is hard to find another technology that can accomplish all we have just stated. There will be thousands of agents in multiple agencies, with superagents that will filter, search, locate, adapt, and make intelligent decisions on the data with which they are presented, according to a predefined strategy or the rules of the corporation.

# APPENDIX

# Bots

*Copernic:* Copernic is an intelligent agent that carries out your net-searches by consulting simultaneously the most important search engines on the Web. It features a history of your searches, making sure that the precious information found on the Internet is always classified and handy. (9/25/97)

*ZurfRider:* ZurfRider is a state-of-the-art World Wide Web search bot. ZurfRider calls out in parallel, and the best search engines on the Internet merges the results, removes redundancies, automatically groups the results into neat, understandable folders, and then asks you questions in simple English to help you narrow down your search. (9/25/97)

*JESS (Java Expert System Shell):* The Java Expert System Shell (JESS) is a clone of the CLIPS expert system shell. JESS was written entirely in Sun's Java language by Ernest Friedman-Hill at Sandia National Laboratories in Livermore, California. (9/20/97)

*Messenger:* Messengers are autonomous flows of control that can spawn across the network. This site collects information about messengers and domains where this programming paradigm is applied. (9/14/97)

*Search Broker:* The Search Broker focuses your Web search by giving the subject of your query as the first word. You can consult the list of over 400 subjects. The Search Broker will automatically send the rest of your query to the search engine that specializes in that subject. (9/14/97)

*The Frankfurt Mobile Agents Infrastructure:* The Frankfurt Mobile Agents Infrastructure (ffMAIN) implements an infrastructure for mobile agents that provides for agent mobility across heterogeneous networks as well as communications among agents. It has diverse programming languages and lets agent programmers implement a variety of interaction schemes based on a basic but general communication mechanism. (9/14/97)

*LikeMinds:* LikeMinds is focused on introducing purchase decision agent software that helps people decide what to look at, what to sample, what to try, and what to buy. (9/13/97)

*Personal WebWatcher Project:* The Personal WebWatcher Project is a "personal" agent that accompanies you from page to page as you browse the Web, highlighting hyperlinks that it believes will be of interest. Its strategy for giving advice is learned from feedback from earlier tours.

*WiseWire:* WiseWire Service acts as your personal assistant, combing every inch of the Internet, weeding out the "junk," and looking for interesting material specifically relevant to you. This assistant begins by looking for what other like-minded people have found valuable. Then, with your feedback, it learns to retrieve information customized to your individual interests. (9/13/97)

*World Wide Knowledge Base Project:* The goal of CMU's World Wide Knowledge Base Project is to develop a probabilistic, symbolic knowledge base that mirrors the content of the World Wide Web. If successful, this will make text information on the Web available in computer-understandable form, enabling much more sophisticated information retrieval and problem solving. (9/13/97)

*Yeti:* Yeti—the Abominable Snowman—is a mythical creature that is supposed to live in the Himalayas, the highest mountain range in the world. Although there have been many reported sightings of the Yeti, none of them have been documented with evidence in any way. In terms of description, the Yeti is similar to the North American BigFoot and the African 2nd Gorilla. Here you can talk to the computer-simulated Yeti. The program is an adaptation of the original Eliza and is written in Perl. (9/13/97)

*Java Web Spider:* The Java Web Spider / Search Engine Class is a class to show all the links contained in one URL, a class to recursively display links on a URL structure, a class to turn output into a search engines index and an Applet to search on a previously generated index. The classes and their source are contained in a zip file available for immediate download. (9/11/97)

*CollaWorld Multiagent Collaboration Simulator:* CollaWorld is a simulator that provides insights into how independent agents work with each other in cyber space. (9/09/97)

# 2

# JATLite, a Tool for Developing Agents Created by Stanford University

JATLite (Java Agent Template, Lite) is a package of programs written in the Java language that allows users to create quickly new software "agents" that communicate robustly over the Internet. JATLite provides a basic infrastructure in which agents register with an Agent Message Router facilitator, using a name and password, connect/disconnect from the Internet, send and receive messages, transfer files, and invoke other programs or actions on the various computers where they are running.

JATLite especially facilitates construction of agents that send and receive messages using the emerging standard communications language, KQML (see http://www.cs.umbc.edu/kqml/ for the current KQML standard). The communications are built on open Internet standards, TCP/IP, SMTP, and FTP. However, developers may easily build agent systems using other agent languages that use JATLite.

What is JATLite good for?

Agent systems are difficult to build and debug from scratch. And new agent systems should be built in Java so that agents can run on heterogeneous platforms and make use of very lightweight applets as temporary agents. JATLite provides a ubiquitous Java agent platform that makes it easy to build systems in a common way, but without imposing any particular theory of autonomous agents—thus the "Lite" in JATLite.

JATLite provides a template for building agents that utilize a common high-level language and protocol. This template provides the user with numerous predefined Java classes that facilitate agent construction. Furthermore, the classes are provided in layers, so that the developer can easily decide what classes are needed for a given system. For instance, if the developer decides not to use KQML, the classes in the KQML layer are simply omitted. However, if that layer is included, parsing and other KQML-specific functions are automatically included.

JATLite does not endow agents with specific capabilities beyond those needed for communication and interaction. In particular, JATLite does not, by itself, construct "intelligent agents" that seek information or automate human tasks, as discussed in the artificial intelligence community. The developer is left free to use whatever theories and techniques are best suited for the targeted application or research.

However, JATLite does provide a robust substrate for building such intelligent agents. The JATLite packaged infrastructure allows agents to be portable (for example, on a laptop computer), to move from one machine to another, and to connect and disconnect from the Internet with automatic queuing and buffering of incoming messages. These features, found to be necessary for robust agent behavior in projects in which software agents occasionally fail or migrate, are provided by the Agent Message Router (AMR) infrastructure.

This unique facility also overcomes Netscape security restrictions on applets, allowing them to be full-fledged but highly migratory lightweight agents. Applet agents can be run from any browser: There is no need for any specialized "docking" software to be installed.

What are the potential applications?

A primary application of JATLite is to "wrap" existing programs by providing them with a front end that allows them automatically to communicate with other programs, sending and receiving messages, files, etc. JATLite allows agents to make a single connection to an Agent Message Router (AMR) that buffers messages and handles all IP address information. JATLite provides many useful features. Any agent sending KQML can use the JATLite if the agent is consistent with JATLite assumptions.

A key idea is that even if no new autonomous agents are ever built, agent technology provides a "glue" for composing legacy software. JATLite provides standard software for agent communications. KQML and other agent protocols provide standards for message exchange. Various process analysis systems can then provide guidance for the composition of specific messages among the system agents.

JATLite is tested extensively within the CDR to investigate the composition of engineering software agents for design analysis and optimization, and for the coordination of the design and development process.

It is particularly easy to integrate JATLite with other Java software, but JATLite agents have also been integrated with C + + and Lisp code, albeit without the platform-independent advantages of pure Java.

## TECHNICAL DESCRIPTION

### Summary of Capabilities

Modular construction consisting of layers, each of which can be be exchanged with other technologies without affecting the operation of the rest of the package. Low-level communications based on TCP/IP, as supported by commonly used operating systems (for example, Unix, Windows, and MAC OS). Other protocols (for example, e-mail) can be added easily.

Agent messages based on the KQML language and protocol, with built-in parsing for the outer layer of messages. The inner "contents" of messages can be in any language (for example, SQL, Express, and KIF). Multithreaded operation, with multiple server sockets and message receiver sockets. Socket connections are persistent and have time-out provisions. Provides Message Routers for agent registration, connection, name, and password services. Provides storage and queuing of messages for mobile and sporadic agents. Supports stand-alone agents in Java and C + + , and applet agents through popular WWW browsers (for example, Netscape, Internet Explorer). Built-in FTP file transfer capability.

### Assumptions

JATLite can run on any platform that supports the Java development kit JDK1. 1 from Sun Microsystems, Inc., including Windows95, WindowsNT, Solaris, Mac OS8. Modifications may be needed for other Java environments. Applet agents can be run using a WWW browser such as Netscape or Internet Explorer, or Sun's applet viewer. JATLite agents also utilize standard TCP/IP communications and sockets for interprocess communication. All communications are assumed to take place through Message Routers, which are stand-alone Java programs running on hosts connected to the Internet. Connection details can be found at

http://java.stanford.edu/JATLiteRouter.html#Api

### Architecture

The JATLite architecture is organized as a hierarchy of increasingly specialized layers, so that developers can select the appropriate layer from which to start building their systems. Thus, a developer who wants to utilize TCP/IP communications but does not want to use KQML can use only the Abstract and Base layers as described in the following sections.

The Abstract Layer provides the collection of abstract classes necessary for JATLite implementation. Although JATLite assumes all connections to be made using TCP/IP, one can implement different protocols such as UDP by extending the Abstract Layer.

The Base Layer provides basic communication based on TCP/IP and the Abstract Layer. There is no restriction on the message language or protocol. The

Base Layer can be extended, for example, to allow inputs from sockets and output to files. The Base Layer can also be extended to provide agents with multiple message ports, and so on.

The KQML Layer provides for storage and parsing of KQML messages. Extensions to the KQML standard, proposed by the Center for Design Research (see http://cdr.stanford.edu/ProcessLink/kqml-proposed.html), are implemented to provide a standard protocol for registering, connecting, disconnecting, and so on.

The Router Layer provides name registration and message routing and queuing for agents. All agents send and receive messages via the Router, which forwards them to their named destinations. When an agent intentionally disconnects or accidentally crashes, the Router stores incoming messages until the agent is reconnected. The Router is particularly important for applet agents, which can initiate socket connections only with the host that spawned them, because of WWW and Java security restrictions. On top of Router Layer, Protocol Layer will support diverse standard internet services such as SMTP, FTP, POP3, HTTP, and so on, both for stand-alone applications and for applets. Current beta version supports SMTP and FTP, but other protocols can be easily extended from Protocol Layer. If your agents are expecting to transfer nonsentential, lengthy data or if your agents need to send KQML message through e-mail, Protocol Layer will be a good starting point.

As of August 1997, JATLite is being used or evaluated for creating agent interfaces for a variety of applications, including commercial CAD software (AutoCad ARX14), decision and dependency tracking programs (Redux), constraint management (CM, ProcessLink), rapid prototyping services (Cybercut, RPL), prototypical financial analysis agents, information searching and retrieval agents, ship design and construction, and so on.

# 3

# Foundations of Objects

The following elements form the foundation of the object system.

*Abstraction:* An abstraction allows us to focus on the important functions of an object. Gooch gives the example of a thermometer in a greenhouse. The most important function is that if asked to do so, the thermometer will return a temperature. Another important function is that we can calibrate the thermometer.

*Encapsulation:* By encapsulation, we mean the hiding of none of the essential details. To measure temperature, a thermometer might use the heat coefficients of metal, but that process is not directly relevant to its task. Therefore, in describing the process, we only confuse a potential user by explaining it. Encapsulation and abstraction are twins.

*Modularity:* All things are objects from the earth, down to a discrete particle. Modularity allows objects to be made up of other objects.

*Hierarchy:* In hierarchies, a major concept of objects is demonstrated. Objects can inherit. Because of this inheritance capability, we can define "classes" of objects. Mammals have specific properties: they are warm-blooded, have backbones, and bear live young. People are a subclass of mammals and therefore inherit all these characteristics plus the things that make people unique. Through hierarchies, we do not need to describe every property of an object, only the things that differentiate the subclass from the class. The idea of inheritance leads inexorably to the concept of classes of objects. A class is a set of objects that share a common structure and a common behavior.

# 4

# JAFMAS, an Agent Development System

## JAFMAS, A JAVA-BASED AGENT FRAMEWORK FOR MULTIAGENT SYSTEMS DEVELOPMENT AND IMPLEMENTATION

### Abstract

The Java-based Agent Framework for Multiagent Systems (JAFMAS) provides a generic methodology for developing speech-act-based multiagent systems (MAS), an agent architecture, and a set of classes to support implementing these agents in Java. The methodology follows five stages: (1) identifying the agents, (2) identifying the conversations, (3) identifying the conversations rules, (4) analyzing the conversation model, and (5) MAS implementation. JAFMAS provides communication, linguistic, and coordination support through sixteen Java classes. Communication support is provided for both directed communication and subject-based broadcast communication. This feature enables the user to develop scalable, fault-tolerant, self-configurable and flexible multiagent systems.

Linguistic support is provided through speech-act-based (for example, KQML) communication language that provides an agent-independent semantics. Coordination support follows from Carl Searle's thesis (*Speech Acts,* Cambridge University Press, 1962) that "speaking a language is engaging in a (highly complex) rule-governed form of behavior." We conceptualize agent plans and their coordination as rule-based conversations represented by automata models. JAFMAS classes support each agent with multiple threads, one for the agent, one for each conversation in which the agent engages, and one for each subject to which the agent subscribes. Though JAFMAS provides sixteen Java classes, the user needs to extend just four of these classes to develop a multiagent application. A five-step process is presented for implementing a multiagent system. Here JAFMAS classes are extended for each agent, for each conversation, for each conversation rule, and for an operator interface to develop application-specific classes. Then a start-up procedure is designed. Multiagent application development, using JAFMAS, is demonstrated through example applications of the N-Queens problem and supply chain integration. Petri Net–based analysis tools are used to determine conversation coherency in each MAS.

Comparisons are provided between JAFMAS and other Java-based tools supporting speech-acts (JATLite, Java-based tools supporting mobile agents (IBM Aglets, Concordia, Odyssey, Voyager), and other agent-building tools that are not Java-based (COOL, InteRRap, dMars, Cybele, Telescript, AgentTcl, Swarm, and Echelon).

# Agents Currently Listed by the Agent Society as Being Developed

**AgentSoft**
Product: Live Agent
Product: LiveAgent Pro

**Andersen Consulting, Center for Strategic Technology Research, Knowledge technologyAndersen**
Consulting - Knowledge Technologies
Service: Bargain Finder
Service: Lifestyle Finder

**AutoNomy**
Product: AutoNomy

**Botspot, Inc.**
Service: Botspot

**British Telecom**
Research: Jasper
Research: Distributed cooperative agents for service management in communications networks
Outsourced research: Customer process control

**Broadvision**
Product: One-to-One (profile and community management objects)

**Bunyip Information Systems, Inc.**
Product: client Silk
Technology: Uniform Resource Agents

**Charles River Analytics**
Service: OpenSesame

**Corporation for National Research Initiatives**
Service: Knowbot Information Service (KIS)
Client: Grail
Language: Python

**Crystaliz, Inc.**
Product: LogicWare
Technology: Mubots

**DEC**
Language: Obliq

**Firefly Network, Inc.**
Service: Firefly
Product: Profile and community management objects

**FTP Software, Inc.**
Product: Product development

**Fujitsu**
Research: Advanced Software Lab
Language: AprilQ + +

**General Magic:**
Product: Odyssey
Paper: Mobile Agents White Paper

**Guideware Corp:**
Products: personal agents, enterprise agents
Language: A Visual Language (AVL)

**Home Buyer:**
Product: Distributed intelligent agent applications

**IBM:**
Service: InfoMarket
Research: Agent home page

Research: David Chess, TJ Watson, Massively Distributed Systems
IBM Japan, product: Aglets—mobile java agents

**Intelligent Agent Group:**
Research:

**Javasoft:**
Technique: Remote Method Invocation for Java $^{TM}$
Standard: Java Servlet Application Programming Interface

**Kinetoscope, Inc.:**
Service: Quantico Agentbase

**KYMA Software, Inc.:**
Product: KYMA-Atlantis

**Locheed:**
Research: Artificial Intelligence Center

**Microelectronics and Computer Technology Corporation:**
Project: Carnot

**Microsoft:**
Platform: ActiveX
Product: Microsoft agent

**Microstrategy:**
Service: Intelligent agents

**The Mining Co.:**
Service: Software agents

**Mitsubishi:**
Product: Concordia

**NetAngels.com, Inc.:**
Product: AngelMarks (client personal profiling)

**NETbot, Inc.:**
Product: MetaCrawler
Product: Ahoy

**NTT Communication Science Laboratories:**
Language: AgenTalk: Describing Multiagent Coordination Protocols

**ObjectSpace:**
Product: Voyager

**Open Group (OSF):**
Project: Mobile Objects and Agents Project (MOA)

**Oracle:**
Service: Mobile agents

**Personal Agents, Inc.:**
Description of "Intelligent Agent standard"

**Price Waterhouse Technology Centre:**
Individual research: Scot Huffman

**Quarterdeck/Limbex:**
Product: Webcompass

**Softbots, Inc.:**
Product: Browser buddy

**Sun Microsystems:**
Project, language: Tcl/Tk

**Tierra:**
Product: Tierra Highlights

**Unisys:**
Product: KQML

**Verity:**
Product: Topic Agent

**Webcrawler:**
Product: Robots, wanderers, and spiders

**Wireless Connect:**
Potential wireless application

**Xerox PARC:**
Dynamics of multiagent systems

# 6

# Los Alamos Lab's "Killer Agent"

Robots Beware

Effective 1 Jan '96: "We attack back."

This WWW server has been under all-too-frequent attack from "intelligent agents" (a.k.a. "robots," and more recently, "accelerators") that mindlessly download every link encountered, ultimately trying to access the entire database through the listings links. In most cases, these processes are run by well-intentioned but thoughtless neophytes, ignorant of commonsense guidelines.

(Very few of these same robotrunners would ever dream of downloading entire databases via anonymous ftp, but for some reason conceptualize www sites as somehow associated only to small and limited databases. This mentality must change—large databases such as this one [which has millions of distinct URL's that lead to gigabytes of data] are likely to grow ever more commonly exported via WWW).

Following a proposed standard for robot exclusion, this site has maintained since early '94 a file/robots.txt that specifies those URL's that are off-limits to robots. (And this "Robots Beware" page was originally posted March 1994.)

We are not willing to play sitting duck to nonsensical methods of "indexing" information. (Presumably you neither would be terribly thrilled if every aspiring encyclopedia editor were to send a gang of blind 600 lb gorillas to your library, armed with a photocopy machine.) We also have no intention of inconveniencing in any way our many tens of thousands of real users, just because a small handful of misconfigured miscreants—with neither interest in, nor understanding of, our actual content—is incapable of abiding by well-posted guidelines.

This server is configured to monitor activity and deny access to sites that violate the above guidelines. Continued rapid-fire requests from any site after access has been denied (i.e. with 403 Access denied HTTP response) will be interpreted as a network attack; and we will respond accordingly—without hesitation, and without further warning.

(Click here to initiate automated "seek-and-destroy" against your site.)

If some specific application requires relaxation of the above guidelines, contact www-admin@xxx.lanl.gov in advance of any attempted download. This system is not responsible for the consequences of automated downloads attempted in violation of the above guidelines.

return to xxx

www-admin@xxx.lanl.gov

# APPENDIX

## 7

# Cookies

Cookies are early examples of level-three agents. This description of their capabilities gives the reader a flavor of this agent tool.

The WWW is built on a very simple, but powerful, premise. All material on the Web is formatted in a uniform format called HTML (Hypertext Markup Language), and all information requests and responses conform to a similarly standard protocol. When someone accesses a server on the Web, such as the Library of Congress, the user's Web browser will send an information request to the Library of Congress's computer. This computer is called a Web server. The Web server will respond to the request by transmitting the desired information to the user's computer. There, the user's browser will display the received information on the user's screen.

Cookies are pieces of information generated by a Web server and stored in the user's computer, ready for future access. Cookies are embedded in the HTML information, flowing back and forth between the user's computer and the servers. Cookies were implemented to allow user-side customization of Web information. For example, cookies are used to personalize Web search engines, to allow users to participate in WWW-wide contests (but only once!), and to store shopping lists of items that a user has selected while browsing through a virtual shopping mall.

Essentially, cookies make use of user-specific information transmitted by the Web server onto the user's computer so that the information might be available for later access by itself or other servers. In most cases, not only does the storage of personal information into a cookie go unnoticed, so does access to it. Web servers automatically gain access to relevant cookies whenever the user establishes a connection to them, usually in the form of Web requests.

Cookies are based on a two-stage process. First, the cookie is stored in the user's computer without his or her consent or knowledge. For example, with customizable Web search engines like My Yahoo!, a user selects categories of interest from the Web page. The Web server then creates a specific cookie, which is essentially a tagged string of text containing the user's preferences, and it transmits this cookie to the user's computer. The user's Web browser, if cookie-savvy, receives the cookie and stores it in a special file called a cookie list. This process happens without any notification or user consent. As a result, personal information (in this case, the user's category preferences) is formatted by the Web server, transmitted, and saved by the user's computer.

During the second stage, the cookie is clandestinely and automatically transferred from the user's machine to a Web server. Whenever a user directs her or his Web browser to display a certain Web page from the server, the browser will, without the user's knowledge, transmit the cookie containing personal information to the Web server.

What are cookies used for? An example is browser's storing your passwords and user IDS. They are also used to store preferences of start pages; both Microsoft and Netscape use cookies to create personal start pages.

Common cookies that companies use to find information are listed here:

*Online ordering systems:* An online ordering system could be developed, using cookies that would remember what a person wants to buy; this way, if a person spends three hours ordering CDs at your site and suddenly has to get off the net, the person could quit the browser and return weeks or even years later and still have those items in their shopping basket.

*Site personalization:* This is one of the most beneficial uses. Let's say that a person comes to the MSNBC site but doesn't want to see any sports news. Site personalization allows a person to select this as an option; from then on (until the cookie expires), the person wouldn't see sports news. This is also useful for start pages.

*Website tracking:* Site tracking can show you "Dead End Paths," places in your Web site that people go to and then wander off from because they don't have any more interesting links to hit. It can also give you more accurate counts of how many people have been to pages on your site. You could differentiate fifty unique people seeing your site from one person hitting the reload button fifty times.

*Targeted marketing:* This is probably one of the main uses of cookies. They can be used to build up a profile of where you go and what adverts you click on. This information is then used to target adverts at you that companies think are of interest. Companies also use cookies to store which adverts have been displayed so that the same advert does not get displayed twice.

How does security fit in? An HTTP cookie cannot be used to get data from your hard drive, get your e-mail address, or steal sensitive information about your person. Early implementations of Java and JavaScript could allow people to do these things, but for the most part, these security leaks have been plugged. But HTTP cookie can be used to track where you travel over a particular site.

There is a limit of 300 cookies, and a new cookie will delete on an FIFO system the oldest cookie set if it would exceed that count.

# Bibliography

## MOBILITY

External Interfaces Working Group ARPA Knowledge Sharing Effort. KQML Overview. Working Paper, 1992.

Technical Report CS-94-02
Computer Science Department
University of Maryland, UMBC
Baltimore, MD 21228

Tim Finin and Rich Fritzson
Computer Science Department
University of Maryland, UMBC
Baltimore, MD 21228

Don McKay and Robin McEntire
Valley Forge Engineering Center
Unisys Corp.
Paoli, PA 19301

External Interfaces Working Group ARPA Knowledge Sharing Effort. Specification of the KQML Agent-Communication Language. Working paper, December 1992.

S. Bussmann and J. Mueller. A communication architecture for cooperating agents. *Computers and Artificial Intelligence,* 12:37–53, 1993.

M. Cutkosky, E. Engelmore, R. Fikes, T. Gruber, M. Genesereth, and W. Mark. PACT: An experiment in integrating concurrent engineering systems, 1992.

Edmund H. Durfee, Victor R. Lesser, and Daniel D. Corkill. Trends in cooperative distributed problem solving. *IEEE Transactions on Knowledge and Data Engineering,* 1(1):63–83, March 1989.

Tim Finin, Rich Fritzson, and Don McKay. A language and protocol to support intelligent agent interoperability. In Proceedings of the CE & CALS Washington '92 Conference, June 1992.

Tim Finin, Rich Fritzson, and Don McKay, et al. An overview of KQML: A knowledge query and manipulation language. Technical report, Department of Computer Science, University of Maryland, Baltimore County, 1992.

Tim Finin, Don McKay, Rich Fritzson, and Robin McEntire. KQML: an information and knowledge exchange protocol. In International Conference on Building and Sharing of Very Large-Scale Knowledge Bases, December 1993.

Mike Genesereth. Designworld. In *Proceedings of the IEEE Conference on Robotics and Automation,* pages 2,785–2,788. IEEE CS Press, 1997.

M. Genesereth, R. Fikes, et al. Knowledge interchange format, version 3.0 reference manual. Technical report, Computer Science Department, Stanford University, 1992.

Mike Genesereth. An agent-based approach to software interoperability. Technical Report Logic-91-6, Logic Group, CSD, Stanford University, February 1993.

Carl Hewitt and Jeff Inman. DAI betwixt and between: From "intelligent agents" to open systems science. *IEEE Transactions on Systems, Man and Cybernetics,* 21(6), December 1991 (Special Issue on Distributed AI).

Michael N. Huhns, David M. Bridgeland, and Natraj V. Arni. A DAI communication aide. Technical Report ACT-RA-317-90, MCC, Austin, Texas, October 1990.

R. E. Kahn. Digital Library Systems, *Proceedings of the Sixth Conference on Artificial Intelligence Applications CAIA-90* (Volume II: Visuals), Santa Barbara, Calif., pp. 63–64, 1990.

Dan Kuokka et al. Shade: Technology for knowledge-based collaborative. In AAAI Workshop on AI in Collaborative Design, 1993.

Robert MacGregor and Raymond Bates. The Loom Knowledge Representation Language, *Proceedings of the Knowledge-Based Systems Workshop,* St. Louis, Mo., April 1987.

James McGuire et al. Shade: Technology for knowledge-based collaborative engineering. *Journal of Concurrent Engineering: Research and Applications,* to appear.

Don McKay, Tim Finin, and Anthony O'Hare. The intelligent database interface. In *Proceedings of the 7th National Conference on Artificial Intelligence,* August 1990.

R. Neches, R. Fikes, T. Finin, T. Gruber, R. Patil, T. Senator, and W. Swartout. Enabling technology for knowledge sharing. *AI Magazine,* 12(3):36–56, Fall 1991.

Jeff Y-C Pan and Jay M. Tenenbaum. An intelligent agent framework for enterprise integration. *IEEE Transactions on Systems, Man and Cybernetics,* 21(6), December 1991 (Special Issue on Distributed AI).

Mike P. Papazoglou and Timos K. Sellis. An organizational framework for cooperating intelligent information systems. *International Journal on Intelligent and Cooperative Information Systems,* 1(1), 1992.

Jon Pastor, Don McKay, and Tim Finin. View-concepts: Knowledge-based access to databases. First International Conference on Information and Knowledge Management, Baltimore, Md., November 1992.

R. Patil, R. Fikes, P. Patel-Schneider, D. McKay, T. Finin, T. Gruber, and R. Neches. The darpa knowledge sharing effort: Progress report. In B. Nebel, C. Rich, and W. Swartout, editors, *Principles of Knowledge Representation and Reasoning: Proceedings of the Third International Conference* (KR'92), San Mateo, Calif., November 1992. Morgan Kaufmann.

J. R. Searle. What is a speech act? In M. Black, editor, From *Philosophy in America*, pages 221–239. Allen & Unwin, 1965.

## LAW

Lloyd. Liabilities for the contents of on-line services, 3 Int. J. Law & I.T., 1995, 273.

Lloyd. Shopping in Cyberspace, International Journal of Law & Information Technology, 1993, 335.

Lloyd and Simpson. *Law on the Electronic Frontier* (David Hume Institute: Edinburgh 1995). http://www.strath.ac.uk/Departments/Law/diglib/book/front.html

Perritt. Mapping the information superhighway, 3 Int. J. Law & I.T., 1995, 201.

Reed and Davies. *Digital Cash—The Legal Implications.* IT Law Unit, 1995.

Reed, Walden, and Davies. *Electronic Bulletin Boards and the Law.* IT Law Unit, 1995.

Rubin, Fraser, and Smith. US and international law aspects of the Internet, 3 Int. J. Law & I.T., 1995, 117.

Saxby. Public sector policy and the information superhighway, 2 Int. J. Law & I.T., 1994, 221.

Smith (ed.), *Internet Law and Regulation* (FT Law & Tax: London 1996). http://www.twobirds.com/newbook.htm

## EUROPEAN UNION COMPUTER LAW

Clifford Chance. *Information Technology 1992.*

Clifford Chance. *1992—An Introductory Guide.*

T. Hoeren and T. Cowen. EEC computer law (Chapter 12 in Reed).

Copyright Protection for Software—general issues and U.S.

John Reed. EC anti-trust law and the exploitation of intellectual property rights in software. 32 *Jurimetrics Journal,* 1992, p. 431.

Vinje. Licensing software in Europe: EC competition considerations. 1 International Computer Lawyer 3.


## UNITED STATES COMPUTER LAW

J. Baumgarten and C. Meyer. Effects of US adherence to the Berne Convention with particular reference to the protection of computer programs and related works. Cummings Law & Practice, 207.

Broderbund Software v. Unison World Inc. 648 F Supp 1127 (N D Cal 1986).

J. Brown. International trends in computer program protection. 3 CL&P, 1987, 157.

Michael A. Dailey. Digital Communications Associates Inc. v. SoftKlone Distributing Corporation et al: the 'look & feel' of copyrightable expression. EIPR, 1987, 234.

Michael A. Dailey and Henry W. Jones. Whelan Associates Inc. v. Jaslow Dental Laboratory Inc.: the expanding range of copyrightable expression. EIPR, 1987, 50.

G. Gervaise Davis. What hath CONTU wrought? How computer software copyright cases 'look & feel' eight years after the CONTU report (unpublished paper—includes detailed case list and bibliography).

Lotus Development Corporation v. Paperback Software International 740 F. Supp 37 (1990).

Christopher Millard. *Legal Protection of Computer Programs and Data,* Chapter 3.

N.E.C. v. Intel (1989) 10 USPQ 1177.

Nimmer, Bernacchi, and Frischling. A structured approach to analyzing the substantial similarity of computer software in copyright infringement cases. 20 Arizona State Law Journal, 1988, 625.

H. Pearson. Copyright and the Berne Convention: Significant changes for the computer industry. 5 CL&P, 202.

Plains Cotton Cooperative Association v. Goodpasture Computer Services, Inc. 807 F 2d 1256 (5th Cir 1987).

Gary L. Reback et al. The plain truth: Program structure, input formats and other functional works. *The Computer Lawyer* 4(3) March 1987, 1.

G. Schumann. Copyrightability of computer programs and the scope of their protection under the ITC Apple case and the Whelan case. 4 Cummings Law & Practice, 1988, 109, 141.

Richard Stern. Is there, and should there be, infringement of copyright when computer programs written in different codes achieve the same results? EIPR, 1985, 123.

Whelan Associates v. Jaslow Dental Laboratory 797 F.2d 1222 (1986); 609 F.Supp 1307 (1985).

# Index